THE
PENNY PINCHER'S ALMANAC

HANDBOOK
· FOR ·
MODERN
FRUGALITY

Dean King
and
The Editors of *The Penny Pincher's Almanac*

A Fireside Book
Published by Simon & Schuster

New York   London   Toronto   Sydney   Tokyo   Singapore

FIRESIDE

Rockefeller Center
1230 Avenue of the Americas
New York, New York 10020

First Fireside Edition 1992

Designed by John Dernbach
Manufactured in the United States of America

10 9 8 7 6 5 4

The information in this book is not intended to replace or substitute for medical, financial or other professional advice. If you have questions concerning your health, you should consult a doctor or other health care professional.

Library of Congress Cataloging-in-Publication Data

The Penny pincher's almanac handbook for modern frugality
    edited by Dean King and the editors of the Penny Pincher's Almanac
    1st Fireside ed.
            p.   cm.
    "A Fireside book."
    ISBN 0-671-79728-X
    1. Finance, Personal.   2. Saving and thrift.   I. King, Dean
HG179.P363 1993
332.024–dc20   92-35943
                                                              CIP

Table of Contents

Foreword

Here at *The Penny Pincher's Almanac*, we have taken Benjamin Franklin's famous quotation about thriftiness and retooled it for the 1990s: **"A penny saved is worth more than a penny earned."** That's because when you earn a penny, you have to pay upwards of 30% taxes on it. But when you save one, it's all yours. And that's why we have dedicated ourselves to discovering the best ways to save money in today's complex marketplace and around the ever-changing home.

For us, the art of saving money has become a challenge, a mission, a way of life even—but not an obsession. We like to think we are practical about these matters, and that the methods we have developed are useful even in such fast-paced times. Whether you live in the country or in a city, whether you have a house full of kids or are caring for an elderly parent, and even if you quite frequently find yourself working a 60-hour week, there are convenient ways to save money—and time.

For starters, you can shop more intelligently. Did you know that grocery stores put the most expensive products at eye level? Or that if you buy checks from your bank you are paying too much? Do you know the easy technique for buying a new car at just over dealer cost? As any successful athlete can tell you, you must have a game plan to win a competition. In this contest, retailers (as much as we love them) are the opponents. They have plans to sell you the most goods they can, at the highest prices they can. There is nothing wrong with that. But you need to have a plan for buying only what you need and at the best possible price. Sometimes that even means skipping the retailer and going straight to the wholesaler.

But being a wise consumer depends primarily upon gaining a deeper understanding of your family's needs and goals. **Modern-day penny-pinching is more than a practice; it's a new attitude.** Perhaps it's time to check your priorities. Why not try to get another year out of that car? Couldn't you give up a round of golf every other weekend to grow your own vegetables or to cut your own grass with a push mower? And wouldn't that be just as satisfying? How about getting the family to pitch in? Believe it or not, they'll actually enjoy helping out with meals and chores if approached properly.

It's time to rethink old ways of doing things and to consider how you can use your resources more efficiently. The tips and secrets that we pass on to you are the product of much careful observation and thousands of incisive questions by our staff. **Like most good advice, many of our penny-pinching tips fall under the rubric of common sense.** For one reason or another, it is common sense that has been lost to us in recent years.

Take, for instance, some of the wonderfully simple tips we received from the Old Order Amish, a group that has stubbornly clung to its values for some 400 frugal years. Here's one of our favorites: When drying sheets on a line, fasten all four corners, so they'll fill with air like a sail and dry more quickly. (The Amish hang laundry by category and color, and tourists flock to Pennsylvania to take pictures of their beautiful clotheslines!) The Amish also use cut-off plastic milk jugs as plant hothouses in the spring, and they use grass clippings as fertilizer and to keep weeds down.

Not all of our suggestions will be right for you, but some combination almost surely will be. More important is your way of thinking. **Adopting sound financial habits is like learning manners**. You learn them so that when you need them, they come easily and naturally. You become thrifty and resourceful almost without thinking about it.

Today's penny pincher is not the old curmudgeon who has squirreled away so much junk that he can't find anything. (We keep only what we need and have adequate storage space for. Anything more clutters up home and mind.) And *The Handbook for Modern Frugality* is not about sweating over every last detail or making by hand everything you use. **Remember, time is irreplaceable.** It's the one commodity that can't be traded, bartered, exchanged. Ultimately this book is about using resources—time, talent, and money—more efficiently and living in a more fulfilling way. We hope you agree.

—Dean King, *editor*

□ □ □

Thanks to *The Penny Pincher's Almanac* staff: Logan Ward, *managing editor*; Jessica King, *senior editor*; John Dernbach, *art director*; Phil Berney, *associate publisher*; and Wick Allison, *publisher.* And to our contributors: Hank and Marlene Bruce, Winifred Conkling, Betsey King, Geoffrey Morris, Bart Mullin, Richard Nalley, Liz Perkins, Julie Reed, and Kirk Walsh. Special thanks also to John Boswell and Patty Brown for their help and encouragement; to Fireside editor Ed Walters for his careful guidance; and to Simon & Schuster managing editor Suzanne Donahue.

Introduction

Welcome to the 1990s and the new American ethic. The "disposable" society is being transformed back into a can-use, can-do society—one that puts the environment, as well as thriftiness, back on top. As Americans reject the excesses of the past, they rediscover the plain old-fashioned joy of saving money. This new ethos seems destined to outlive the recession that spawned it.

With information on everything from where to buy sporting goods or kitchen utensils wholesale to how to choose the health coverage that's right for your family, *The Handbook for Modern Frugality* maps out money-saving opportunities. You chart the course. For easy use, the handbook is divided into 10 chapters, eight that cover the major areas of family expenditures: food, clothing, home, utilities, auto, health, education, entertainment; and two key chapters on shopping and money management.

At the top of each chapter, a handy table of contents tells you exactly where to find what you need for quick reference. Look for "Inside Advice," which comes from experts—plumbers, auto mechanics, travel agents, farmers, and retailers. They give you the inside scoop like nobody else can. Find out how to beat the rip-offs, how to avoid services you don't need, and how to stay one step ahead of the stores.

Use this information, assess your needs carefully, budget your time and money—and then stick to your guns. You'll be amazed at how the bargains start finding you. Many will seem so obvious that you'll wonder how you ever missed them in the first place. To get you started and to show you how easy it is to save significant amounts of money, we've come up with a quick list of relatively easy savings that add up to a little more than $2,000. (And if you don't think the little things amount to much, take a look at point No. 3.)

Eight-Point Plan for Saving $2,000 This Year

1. The average American family spends $350 on Christmas presents each year. Use our tips for homemade presents beginning on page 160 and the wholesale vendors recommended for compact discs, sporting equipment, and clothing to cut that expense in half. **Save $175.**

2. Ask your utility or state department of energy for a free home-energy checkup. Follow their recommendations (add insulation and stop drafts, replace incandescent light bulbs with energy-savers and fluorescents, and clean air-conditioner fins and filters and refrigerator coils) and **save $275** on heating, cooling, and electric bills this year.

3. Shop for store brands at your grocery store. If you save half as much as we did, it will amount to $750 in a single year. When shopping at the drugstore for the products listed on page 126, switch to store brands. Do this every other month and save $192 this year. **Total savings: $942.**

4. To save on gasoline costs drive your car no faster than the speed limit and keep your tires properly inflated. Replace clogged air filters and old spark plugs. **Save $206.**

5. Drop your kids off at the library for an organized activity every other month and **save $60** on baby-sitting costs.

6. Prevent clogged-up drains and make minor repairs using our "Inside Advice from a Plumber," page 58. **Save $110.**

7. Save by using our advice on one large-ticket item this year: Seed your lawn instead of laying down sod and save $2,410. Use our negotiating tips (page 106) to buy a used car; save $325. Buy your college kid the tuxedo we recommend on page 93 and save $290. **Minimum savings: $290.**

8. Buy *The Penny Pincher's Almanac* ($2.95) at your local newsstand each quarter and save $60 with each copy—**a total of $228** for the year—or get your money back.

The total savings for this short list is more than $2,200. As you can see, you don't have to take great pains to start saving significant amounts of money quickly.

A Family Affair

With practice, a household of four—even with two working parents—shouldn't need to pay for housekeeping help. But all family members must be responsible. The key to creating a frugal household is to get everyone to pitch in because they want to. That means not just assigning chores but explaining why they need to be done and how important each person's contribution is.

Set aside time to work together as a family. That way, being frugal becomes a lesson in teamwork and an example of how a healthy family works together.

Simplify your family's chores. Making the beds, for instance, can be made easy for children. Just have them pull the covers up to the headboard and place their pillow on top. Don't clutter their beds with lots of stuffed animals and extra pillows that have to be removed each night and replaced each day.

A little responsibility goes a long way. Give each family member a laundry basket to throw dirty clothes in; then let them come pick up their baskets of clothes when they're clean. This will start the process of working toward self-reliance.

Start when they're young. To encourage young children to clean up after themselves, make labels with pictures of toys, books, clothes, etc., and display them in the appropriate storage areas. Kids are more likely to put things away if they have fun doing it.

Start a "savings" account. When they're a little older, give your children a "waste not, want not" allowance in addition to their regular allowance. Every time they forget to turn the light off when they leave a room or keep the water running while brushing their teeth, they have to contribute a quarter to the waste-not box.

Saving With Others

One of the best ways to save money is to coordinate efforts with other people. When you share tasks and equipment with family, friends, or neighbors, you not only get the job done in an efficient and economical manner but also invoke a spirit of community that spills over into other parts of your life. Our ancestors didn't hold barn raisings just because they were the fastest way to erect a barn. They didn't join quilting bees just to economize on candles and firewood. They understood that cooperating with others was often the most satisfying—and effective—way of accomplishing a task. You can put that lesson to use by trying the following:

Share equipment. Share machinery and tools with a neighbor. You provide the lawn mower, and he'll provide the leaf blower. You buy the hot-glue gun, and she'll pay for the electric drill. When you share resources, everyone saves money and storage space.

Form a baby-sitting co-op. Instead of paying money for baby-sitters, barter your time with other mothers and fathers. It's easy to set up a baby-sitting co-op, and it's more fun for the kids, too.

Set up a neighborhood watch. Arrange with neighbors to keep an eye on one another's houses—especially when someone is out of town. Contact your local police precinct for pointers and home-security tips.

Organize a summer camp. Instead of sending young children to expensive day camps, get together with four other families to create your own week-long camp. Each couple takes the kids for a day. They can go to the zoo, visit a museum, play games in the backyard, splash in a pool. Most parents will find it as much fun as their kids do—and a lot easier on their pocketbooks.

Share a vacation house. Instead of renting a small beach house just for your family, pair up with friends and get a bigger one. Your vacation will be more relaxing and cost less, too.

When It Doesn't Pay to Skimp...

When dry-cleaning. Never dry-clean one piece of a suit without the other. Subtle color changes may occur.

When contributing to your savings account.

When shopping for a mattress. Invest in a firm mattress. Your back and bankroll will thank you later.

When deciding whether to take a vacation after a year of hard work.

When choosing running shoes. A bad fit, leading to foot, knee, or back injury, will cost you more in the long run.

When buying toilet paper.

When paying an agreed-upon sum for an honest job well done.

When buying a first home. Think ahead and invest in the proper number of bedrooms. Not doing so is one of the most common reasons for having to sell a house in a down market.

Chapter 1

Shopping Strategies

Savings in this chapter...

Are you constantly buying things that need to be repaired or replaced? Do you spend too much and then fret about it? How often do you order something that turns out not to be what you wanted at all? You need shopping savvy. Whether you're buying tomorrow's dinner or next year's vacation, when you put down your money, it's important to feel confident about your choice. The way you shop affects not only your budget but your life-style.

In this chapter you'll learn strategies to use for efficient shopping as well as how to buy for others without having to neglect yourself. We've included a whole section on where to shop (page 12), because the shopping landscape has changed so much in recent years. A generation ago, Filene's was the only bargain basement around, and you could buy clothing seconds only if you worked in the garment industry. All of that has changed, and today's smart shoppers rarely pay the full retail price for anything.

They also take advantage of estate sales, garage sales, flea markets, and even salvage yards. But they know when and where to look, and they arrive armed with the knowledge they need to avoid wasting time on junk. Did you know that one of the best ways to find vintage fixtures and furniture is to contact the salvage yard when an old hotel or other building is being remodeled?

Look for hard advice on negotiating a lower price (page 21), taking advantage of frequent-purchase deals (page 23), and making the best use of coupons (page 24). Find out who tests the myriad products on the market today so you don't have to and where to turn when those products end up not being all that was promised. Shopping can be difficult, but after all, somebody's got to do it!

□ □ □

Shopping With Power

Food, clothing, household supplies, houses themselves: Most of us spend a substantial amount of time shopping—whether we like it or not. Here are a few pointers for making it easier and more effective:

Plan your trips. Coordinate shopping trips so that you make several purchases at once. Keep lists of what you need, and plan your route to save on parking, gas, and time. Try to avoid making trips for just one item.

Be a loner. If others encourage you to buy more than you need, leave them behind. Kids are notorious for grabbing items off supermarket shelves and throwing them into the cart, but best friends also have a way of talking you into that pair of earrings you don't need or that jacket that's too expensive. It's especially easy to acquire discount frenzy, so be cautious in outlets and off-price stores.

Make friends with the sales clerk. If you shop in a certain store often, it pays to get to know a salesperson there. Once a salesperson becomes familiar with your taste—and budget—he or she can save you time and money by calling you when something you would like comes into the store and by alerting you to upcoming sales.

Warranty care. When you buy appliances, send in the warranty cards. That way you'll find out about defects or recalls. But if you want to cut down on the number of mailings you receive, don't fill out the questions about life-style, age, income, and so forth—they're used by manufacturers to create mailing lists.

Christmas bargains. Catalog prices are fixed about six to nine months before Christmas. So if there is a sudden increase in prices preceding the holidays, shop from catalogs. Conversely, if there is a downturn in the economy and retailers are discounting, you'll find better bargains at the stores.

After Christmas. Take advantage of big post-holiday savings— and get a jump on next year. Shop for wrapping paper, holiday cards and decorations, and other seasonal items.

Spell it out. When ordering furniture, major appliances, or other large items, find out what is included in the shipping costs before you agree to the purchase. Some firms charge extra for interior delivery, uncrating, and assembly. Try to negotiate free delivery.

Shopping overseas. Rather than running out to cash a traveler's check when you're shopping abroad, use your credit or charge card. Most banks and charge-card companies use a wholesale market rate to convert overseas purchases, saving you more than the 1% conversion fee they charge. For more information on using credit cards wisely, see page 138.

Shopping for Others: Gift Giving That Won't Break the Bank

At Christmas, the average American family spends more than $350 on gifts for family and friends. Add to that a year's worth of presents for birthdays, weddings, graduations, and so forth, and you have a gift budget that can get seriously out of line. But you don't have to be a scrooge to trim your costs. Here is some gift-shopping advice:

Double your pleasure. For a year-long gift to your spouse that you'll both enjoy, give a membership to a museum or a magazine subscription.

Buy the book. As a graduation, wedding, or retirement gift, buy a blank book and have the recipient's family and friends, plus teachers, wedding attendants, or coworkers, write notes and paste in pictures. It will mean a lot more than something you can buy, and you'll have fun doing it.

Plan on serendipity. Designate a storage space (away from prying eyes) for gifts, and buy presents when you find good deals, rather than going out and searching for specific items. You'll be able to afford nicer gifts, and you'll save time and money, too.

Pass it on. If someone gives you a present that you cannot use or return, save it to give as a gift later. Just be sure to tag it with the name of the giver so that you don't accidently give it back to that person.

□ □ □

Where to Shop

You might do most of your shopping in a single large department store, but no one source can serve all of your needs. Become familiar with a wide variety of stores and get to know which offer the best bargains for you.

Department stores. They offer convenient, one-stop shopping but generally not the lowest prices. Weigh the time/money equation carefully and try to hit the storewide clearance sales just after Christmas, Easter, and the Fourth of July.

Specialty stores. You won't find large selections or the lowest price tags at small specialty stores or boutiques. But if you find one that consistently carries merchandise you like, it can be a gold mine in saved time—especially because specialty stores are often located in neighborhood shopping centers.

Chain stores. At most shopping centers around the country, you'll find some combination of The Gap, Banana Republic, Benetton, The Pottery Barn, Crate & Barrel, Conran's, The Workbench, and similar stores. Because such chains move so much merchandise, they usually offer very reasonable prices. They also tend to have frequent sales. Use them as a source for such basics as jeans, T-shirts, place mats, and picture frames.

Discount stores. They run the gamut from Pathmark to Wal-Mart. Most carry inexpensive merchandise at inexpensive prices. Don't shop in them for long-lasting or high-quality items, but do buy staples here at bargain prices.

Off-price stores. Stores like Filene's Basement, Loehmann's, Marshalls, T.J. Maxx, and Syms are known in the clothing industry as off-price stores, and their number is increasing by leaps and bounds. Off-price stores keep costs low by buying up manufacturer's over runs, canceled orders, closeouts, remainders, slightly irregular items, and inexpensive copies. They are usually located in areas that don't demand premium rents, and some won't accept credit cards or returns. You won't find high-end amenities such as private dressing rooms, luxurious surroundings, and free alterations. But you are likely to find name-brand and designer clothes (often with the labels cut out) at discounts of up to 75%.

Factory outlets. In the last decade, outlet shopping has become enormously popular. It's not surprising when you consider that it's an arrangement that benefits seller and buyer. Manufacturers bypass retailers and make bigger profits, and consumers avoid retail markups and save up to 75%. Outlets are where manufacturers (including top design houses) unload overruns, canceled orders, samples, and slightly damaged items (or seconds). Outlets exist for just about everything, including clothes, shoes, lingerie, luggage, linens, china, food, kitchenware, books, jewelry, and cosmetics. Be extra careful about inspecting what you buy—as well as avoiding bargain fever—because most don't accept returns.

Outlets are located off the beaten path, away from high-rent districts. More and more often, they're clustered together in outlet centers. Several books can help you find outlet locations. Iris Ellis has been publishing guides to outlet shopping since 1972. She currently offers *Supershopper Diary* ($5), a bare-bones listing of factory-outlet stores and centers, and *Fabulous Finds: The Sophisticated Shopper's Guide to Factory Outlet Centers* ($12.95), which contains some tourist information. To order, send a check for the cover price plus $3 for shipping (for each book) to Iris Ellis, 9109 San Jose Boulevard, Jacksonville, FL 32257. For information, call 904-733-8877.

The Globe Pequot Press publishes a *Factory Outlet Guide* series by "A. Miser" and "A. Pennypincher" that covers New England, the Mid-Atlantic, and the South ($8.95 each). Each guide contains detailed information about factory outlets in the region. A few distributor's outlets (stores that sell products from various manufacturers below retail) and off-price stores are also included.

Warehouse stores. No-frills warehouse stores, like the Price Club and Sam's Club, specialize in bulk-rate merchandise. They are located in huge industrial spaces, usually accept only cash, and provide no baggers (or even bags) for your groceries and other items. Some are clubs and charge an annual fee. Warehouse stores are able to offer low prices because they negotiate deals with wholesalers, which also explains why they don't offer much variety in brand or size and why

Bargain-Hunting in New York City

The Big Apple has a reputation for gouging visitors, but it's also a bargain shopper's mecca. You might even find it's worth planning a trip for the express purpose of saving money. So don your sneakers and get shopping already, will ya?

Discount Department Stores

Century 21 Department Store. 22 Cortland Street (between Church and Broadway), 212-227-9092. Brand-name clothing for men, women, and children. Don't miss the shoe department. One caveat: no dressing rooms (but returns are accepted).

Syms. 42 Trinity Place, 212-797-1199. Clothing for the whole family at great prices—especially good for luggage, outerwear, and shoes.

Daffy's. 335 Madison Avenue, 212-557-4422; and 111 Fifth Avenue, 212-529-4477. Designer clothes and accessories for men, women, and children.

Women's Clothing

S&W. 165 West 26th Street, 212-924-6656. Designer brands: sportswear, outerwear, bags, shoes. Four end-of-season sales each year.

Dress Den Factory Outlet. 601 West 26th Street, 17th floor, 212-727-9200. Thousands of quality brand dresses for $30 plus tax per dress. Returns are accepted with a receipt. Take a taxi—this isn't a great neighborhood.

Men's Clothing

Moe Ginsburg. 162 Fifth Avenue, 212-242-3482. Five floors of great buys on suits, sport coats, trousers, ties, overcoats, shoes. You'd be surprised at who buys suits here! Top American and European brands.

BFO. 149 Fifth Avenue, 212-254-0059. Right across the street from Moe Ginsburg, BFO carries the same kind of merchandise at similar prices. Hit them both.

Electronics and Cameras

Know what you want and the lowest advertised price, and don't buy anything off the street. Shop in these neighborhoods:

Audio/Video: 45th Street, mostly between Fifth Avenue and Broadway.

Computers: Herald Square (approximately Sixth Avenue to Broadway from 30th to 34th Streets).

Cameras: Roughly 17th to 23rd Streets between Park and Seventh Avenues. Top photographers shop at B&H Photo (119 West 17th Street, 212-807-7474).

they don't maintain a consistent stock. If you have ample storage space and can make use of jumbo jars of mayonnaise and gigantic drums of laundry detergent, then you can rake in big savings. In addition to food and household items, most also carry books, gardening supplies, and auto supplies.

Clothing consignment shops. Consignment shops serve a dual purpose. They provide reasonably priced apparel in good condition and allow you to sell clothing you no longer wear. Most pay you half of what they sell the garment for and are fairly picky about what they accept: They prefer clothes to be under three years old and without stains, tears, or missing buttons. Many of these stores are in wealthy areas and have an abundance of designer labels. It certainly pays to make use of a good consignment store as a buyer and a seller.

□ □ □

The Catalog Craze

Catalog shopping has taken the country by storm. Consumers love the ease of shopping from home, on their own schedule, without having to fight for a parking space. In addition, catalogs make it simple to comparison-shop. And it's often economical, too. You avoid paying sales tax if the mail-order company doesn't have any stores in your state; and if the company operates solely through a catalog, its low overhead translates into lower prices.

But shopping by phone or mail does have drawbacks, too. The worst is that you can't see or try on what you've bought until it arrives. Almost all catalog houses accept returns, but you have to factor in the potential cost and inconvenience of sending an item back when you're deciding whether it's worth its price. Always check the guarantee and return policy before ordering. And, to avoid impulse purchases, wait several days before you place an order.

Some of the best things to buy by catalog are items you've seen in stores or use regularly. Food, gardening supplies, audio- and videocassettes, and books are other products that seldom need to be returned. Check out some of the catalogs listed below and look for more bargain catalogs in each chapter of this book.

Baby products. The Right Start Catalog contains just about everything you could need for your baby—at prices that will make you smile. Call 800-548-8531 for a free catalog.

Catalog of sales. Here's a catalog you'll like: Grande Finale ($3 per year), 800-955-9595. It offers closeouts from a variety of quality catalogs (everything from designer clothes to toys) with markdowns from original prices of up to 70%.

Music. Save time and money by ordering compact discs from Noteworthy Music, which offers 12,000 CDs, from classical and big-band to country and rock. It gets the music the same day stores do. This is no club, just rock-bottom prices. Call 603-881-5729 for a free catalog.

Office supplies. Save up to 78% with the Viking Office Products Catalog on everything from pencils to fax machines. Free delivery for orders of $25 or more. Call 800-421-1222 for a free copy.

Pets. Save up to 50% on food, medicine, grooming aids, and other supplies from United Pharmacal Company. For the free catalog—with items for dogs, cats, birds, rabbits, hamsters, gerbils, and horses—call 816-233-8800.

Toys. Order from master toy maker Dick Schnacke, and keep your children happy with whimmydiddles, whirligigs, yo-yos, and loads of other wooden folk toys at prices well below those for trendy trinkets. For a free catalog, write Dick Schnacke's Mountain Craft Shop, American Ridge Road, Route 1, New Martinsville, WV 26155.

Sources That List Catalogs

☞ *The Wholesale-by-Mail Catalog* by The Print Project (HarperPerennial, $15) is a compendium of companies that sell goods at an average of at least 30% below retail. It covers just about everything you would want to buy, and it includes useful advice on buying by mail.

☞ *The Kids' Catalog Collection* by Jane Smolik (The Globe Pequot Press, $11.95) is a guide to more than 500 mail-order sources for everything from infant formula to foreign-language tapes.

☞ The Direct Marketing Association's *Great Catalog Guide* lists more than 250 catalogs in 50 product categories. It also provides tips on ordering by phone or mail. For a copy, send $3 to Consumer Affairs Department, Direct Marketing Association, 6 East 43rd Street, New York, NY 10017.

Auction Action

Auctions can be a fun and frugal way to fill your home. Fortunately for the amateur, most auctions—from Peoria to Paris—operate the same way. You get to see an object close up during what's called the previewing, and as long as your bid is registered before the final gavel falls, you have the same chance to score as the dealers. Auctions, particularly on a local level, are frequently underattended, and bargains abound. Call and find out as much as possible about a sale before you attend. You'll want to determine whether the auction house charges a buyer's or seller's premium (the house's 10% cut plus sales tax). Usually it's the latter, and the fee is paid by the consignor, but with a buyer's premium, the fee is added on top of the bid. Check out house rules before the bidding starts. To go home with steals, not lemons, keep the following guidelines in mind, and do your homework before you raise your paddle.

Evaluating and Bidding

It's essential to have a value in mind before the bidding ever starts. Set your top price while thoroughly examining a piece before the sale, preferably the day before. Take the cane-backed chair, for instance, that you happen to notice in a corner at an estate auction. You check the condition, not just by sitting in it, but by turning it upside down and examining it for signs of age, repair, and structural damage. Although it's marked circa 1930, you notice it's constructed with wooden pegs, not nails, and you strongly suspect it's from the mid-19th century. Now you're glad you have a book like *Kovels' Antiques & Collectibles Price List, 1992 Edition* ($13) or David P. Lindquist's *Official Identification and Price Guide to Antiques and Collectibles* ($11.95)—both musts for the bargain hunter—with you to refer to. You check the value of cane chairs from both 1930 and 1850 (you shouldn't expect to pay the 1850 price) and establish a modest but realistic upper limit you're prepared to bid. Stick to it, and you're positioned to pick up a bargain.

You'll increase your chances for spotting a bargain at an auction if you look for items that are not specialties in that particular region. In Sardis, Georgia, for example, you might be the only bidder to recognize that rare piece of Art Deco glassware. But if you're looking for Windsor chairs, forget it. So is everyone else.

Another good strategy is to bottom-skim. That is, you not only set top limits for items you really want, but also price bottoms for marginal lots. If the bidding for a so-so lot is low, then join in—up to your bottom price. But be sure you have a use for the items. A turntable that once cost $600 isn't a bargain at $10 if you play only CDs now.

Be careful, of course, not to get caught up in bidding fever; never chase an auction lot in excitement. And remember, often the crowd becomes sated and peters out at the end of an auction. This is when you should be most alert for a bargain.

Government auctions. To find out about auctions of surplus goods by the United States government, call 703-537-7796. For guidelines on buying surplus "personal property," write DRMS-NC, 2163 Airways Boulevard, Memphis, TN 38114-5211. The information is free.

Auction info. To find out about auctions and flea markets in a certain region of the U.S., call the Antique Show Hot Line (900-903-7469). Calls cost $1.49 per minute and take three to four minutes.

Sizing Up Secondhand Sales

Finding the roses among the thorns at flea markets, yard sales, and thrift shops is never easy. Sometimes it just takes dumb luck to pluck a gem. But if you prepare, you'll have a much better chance. And, if nothing else, by learning how to size up a sale fast, you'll keep from wasting time and avoid the fool's gold. So how do you find the gems in the junk? Before we give you specific tips, let's differentiate between the various hunting grounds.

Flea Markets

Flea markets vary greatly in size—and quality of merchandise. You'll find everything from true antique markets to roadside junk sales. For help in sorting out the thousands of flea markets across the country, consult *Flea Markets by State* ($6.95). (To order, contact Tanner's Directories, Box 1197, Ellaville, GA 31806; 813-644-4953.)

Inside Advice ✓   ## From Flea-Market Pros

Never buy from a dealer you don't trust. If you're buying jewelry, especially a wedding ring, get references and check to see whether other customers have been satisfied with purchases.

For the best buys, look for smaller dealers but not ones who deal exclusively in some collector's item. Here's what you should look for:

Sheffield silver. Since sterling silver is so expensive these days, many young couples are buying the silver-coated nickel plate known as Sheffield instead. With Sheffield you get good quality at a fraction of sterling's cost.

Household items. Shop for household items (plates, pots and pans, and so forth) at house sales and rummage sales. Estate and house sales are listed in the newspaper classifieds. Arrive early, and you'll often find unused items, like a brand-new set of bath towels.

Eyeglasses frames. Buy eyeglasses frames from flea markets. Old frames are in style and can save you more than $75 on designer frames. Replace the lenses with your prescription.

Leather. Leather is a good item to look for at flea markets because it's particularly expensive new. Well-cared-for quality items hold up for a long time, and aged leather often looks better than new.

Craftsmanship. Look for unusual and highly skilled craftsmanship —something you pay a premium for in new items. You're likely to find a high ratio of well-crafted used items at good flea markets because poorly made products have been eliminated by use.

Yard Sales

Why are some better than others? As the real-estate gurus say— location, location, location. States like New York, Ohio, Michigan, Minnesota—much of the northern U.S., in fact—are the prime picking areas. Why? Because their citizens tend to stay put. People who have lived in one place—particularly the same house—for a long time are much more likely to have valuable things to rid themselves of. The Northeast also has a great concentration of wealth.

Although some people argue that it's best to hit a sale the morning it opens to have a chance at the top merchandise, others wait until the second day because that's when sellers cut prices and are more open to negotiation. A true bargain shopper would probably go at the beginning and categorize the items into must-haves and worth-waiting-to-negotiate-fors.

Thrift Stores

At thrift stores, such as those run by The Salvation Army, Goodwill Industries, and other charity organizations, you never know what you might find. Some consistently receive good-quality donations and others are hit-or-miss. Some of the best are run by churches in affluent neighborhoods. But most are worth your while only if you truly enjoy the hunt—you'll spend a lot of time rummaging through other people's castoffs before you unearth the deal of a lifetime. Keep an eye out for special sales in support of a cause. The Junior League, for instance, often sponsors weekend drives that offer high caliber merchandise donated by its members.

How to Hunt for Secondhand Bargains

Get up early and move fast. Try to beat the crowds, but if you don't, remember that people tend to go right for the furniture, leaving the small collectibles and nice framed prints less picked-over. Good frames, even with bad art in them, are worth more than the few dollars you're likely to pay for them.

Know in detail what you're looking for. And carry a reference guide so you know what you're looking at. Uneducated hunters don't find bargains because they aren't able to recognize one when they see it! For instance, clear and colored Heisey glass from the 1920s through 1940s is very collectible. Many recognize its mark—the little "H" in the diamond—but they don't know that many pieces of Heisy are unmarked. Take a little time to study the different Heisy patterns—so that you recognize them even if they're covered in dust—and increase your chances of finding overlooked pieces.

Don't be afraid to pull the trigger. When you find a truly underpriced item that you really want, don't let it rest—buy. The perennial hard-luck story in antiquing is about the steal that got away. We don't know how many times we've heard it!

From an Antiques Dealer

Inside Advice ✓

Avoid trendy items. Pine furniture, for example, has recently been the rage. It would be a mistake to think that vendors aren't aware of this. Stay away from those items and shop smartly for classics. Here's a start:

☞ **"Made in" stamp.** The U.S. introduced legislation in 1891 forcing countries like Japan and England to put the ubiquitous "Made in" stamps on the products they exported. This makes dating 20th-century pieces like cloisonné vases and Wedgwood earthenware relatively easy.

☞ **Marriage not desired.** If two parts of an object—the top and bottom of a porcelain sugar bowl, for instance—are marked, the markings should match up. "Married" pieces—ones that didn't originate together— often look remarkably compatible. That sugar bowl might have an impressed mark on the lid and a painted mark on the bowl. This, perhaps coupled with the fact that the lid doesn't fit exactly flush, lets you know that the two did not originate together.

☞ **Silver mettle.** Familiarize yourself with the names and stamps of the major historical American and English makers, like Gorham, Barker Ellis, Towle, and Reed & Barton, by buying a book of old marks, such as *The Book of Old Silver* by Seymour B. Wyler (Crown Publishers, $25) or *Jackson's Hallmarks: English, Scottish, Irish* by Ian Pickford (Antique Collectors Club Ltd, $25).

☞ **Collector's glass.** *The Collector's Encyclopedia of Depression Glass* by Gene Florence (Collector Books, Box 3009, Paducah, KY 42002 - 3009; $19.95, plus $2 shipping and handling) can help you get to know glass patterns from American Sweetheart to Windsor Diamond. It comes complete with photographs and the prices you can expect to pay.

Shopping Savvy

What you see isn't always what you get when it comes to price tags. There are ways to get what *you* want without paying what *they* want.

How to Negotiate for Practically Everything

Hard times affect not only shoppers but shops, too. More than ever, retailers are willing to shave their markups in order to move merchandise. In fact, many store owners would rather sell you a discounted item than see you walk away empty-handed. But you have to ask—and argue—persuasively. Remember, the worst they can say is no.

Where to bargain. The smaller the store, the better. At chains and department stores, the salespeople have limited freedom. Do negotiate in single-location shops, where you might be helped by the manager or owner, both of whom know the store's markups and how much they can be cut.

What to say. Work your way in smoothly with something like "Gee, I really can't afford it at that price," or "I'd buy it if it were on sale." Haggling shouldn't be confrontational. You'll do your best work with a smile on your face.

How low to go. Decide what you can pay, then offer 10% to 15% less, leaving room for a couple of counteroffers. Keep in mind that 20% off the retail price is generally considered a fair discount. It's important not to insult a merchant right off the bat with a really low-ball offer. If you anger the seller, he or she will be less likely to come down on the price.

Carry cash. Sellers like cash. Having it can work in your favor if the price is negotiable. A bargain gained is a bargain lost if the seller doesn't take credit cards or checks.

Best goods to bargain for. Chances are you'll have the best luck in three areas: big-ticket items, like stereos, cars, and furniture; damaged merchandise, because you can always find the same item without a flaw; and goods that don't move quickly—it might be worth it for the merchant to lower the price just to get rid of that red Naugahyde recliner.

Think on your feet. Like most sports, bargaining requires agility more than brute strength. In other words, if the seller won't budge on the price, have him throw in delivery, an extended warranty, or other extras for free. One example: If you're buying a stereo, ask for cables, speaker wire, and a few blank cassette tapes on the house.

Privacy helps. Try to bargain during slow hours. Curious customers can keep a salesman from offering real discounts.

Do your homework. If you show a salesman another store's advertisement or price quote, he'll know you're serious.

Volume discounts. You stack the deck anytime you buy in bulk.

Talk to friends before you make a big purchase. They just might need the same thing.

Be a Frequent Shopper

The more you shop, the more you'll save—at some establishments. Many stores and restaurants have followed the lead of airlines, hotels, and rental-car companies in rewarding good customers with discounted rates and special rewards. If your favorite shop doesn't have such a program, suggest that it start one. In the meantime, check out these:

☐ If you buy a lot of books, consider joining the **Waldenbooks Preferred Reader Club.** For a $10 annual fee, you get a 10% discount on most purchases, and you earn a point per dollar spent. For every 100 points you accumulate, Waldenbooks sends you a $5 gift certificate. Members can shop at Waldenbooks stores or from a catalog. For more information, call 800-322-2000.

☐ At participating **Subway restaurants**, ask for a **Sub Club Card** and have it stamped every time you buy a sandwich. When you accumulate 12 stamps, the next sub is on the house.

☐ If you live in Washington, DC, Virginia, or Maryland, take advantage of **Safeway's Savings Club.** Membership is free and entitles you to reductions of 10% to 20%, monthly coupons for free or discounted items, and entries in a monthly sweepstakes for free groceries. For information, talk to the manager at your Safeway store (and if you live outside Safeway's eastern region, encourage your local Safeway manager to offer this program at your store).

☐ A lot of **Domino's Pizza** franchises offer frequent-purchase deals. Typically, if you buy six pizzas, you get the seventh one free. Ask when you order.

☐ Many **gourmet coffee stores** give you a free pound of coffee after you've bought 12 pounds. Ask at the shop where you buy coffee to see whether they'll offer you this deal.

Capitalizing on Coupons

More people are cashing in on coupons than ever before. U.S. consumers redeem more than 7 billion coupons per year, saving $4 billion. While the majority of coupons are for household products, smart manufacturers are offering them for all kinds of items. In a random check of *New York Newsday*, we found more than $160 worth of coupons for everything from wild rice and mayonnaise to shampoo and cold medicine. There was even one for an oil change. Coupons are essential to thrifty shoppers in the nineties. If you're not using them, start. If you are, double your efforts. And while you're at it, keep in mind the following tips:

Shop smart. As with any bargain shopping, use coupons only for items that you would have bought anyway. If you buy something simply because it's discounted, you'll end up wasting money rather than saving it.

Clip as you go. Keep scissors near your favorite reading spots so you can clip coupons when you run across them. If you put it aside to do later, it may never get done.

Highlight savings. Underline or circle the important information on coupons—value, expiration date, restrictions—to save time at the cash register.

Organize. Keep track of your coupons by filing them by category. Note on your shopping list the items for which you will be redeeming coupons.

□ □ □

Who Can Help You?

Prudent shopping is a skill, especially when it comes to major purchases. The biggest mistake most people make is not researching a product or service they're about to pay for. Don't cross your fingers and hope the salesman is telling the truth. Arm yourself with knowledge. Learn about the various features and compare manufacturers of what you're going to buy before you shop. Not only will you have a better idea of what you want, but salespeople shoot straight with educated shoppers.

Consumers Union

The best resource for researching just about any kind of product, from deodorant to minivans, is *Consumer Reports*. This monthly magazine—which, in order to avoid bias, accepts no advertising—is published by Consumers Union, a nonprofit organization established in 1936 to provide information and advice to consumers. At its 180,000-square-foot testing facility in Yonkers, New York, staff members evaluate some 1,500 products each year. The results are printed in *Consumer Reports*, its best-known publication, and in the newer *Zillions*, a children's magazine dedicated to making kids informed consumers. Consumers Union also publishes two monthly newsletters, *On Health* and *Travel Letter*.

Almost all public libraries carry *Consumer Reports*. For subscription information, call 800-234-1645. To find out which back issue has information on a product or service you need, call Consumers Union Product Information at 914-378-2740. Back issues cost $4. Consumers Union also publishes an extensive range of specialized books with specific brand information and ratings on everything from gems to fast food. Annual buying guides and books on cars and electronics can be found in most bookstores. For a complete list of books, or to order directly, contact Consumer Reports Books (9180 LeSaint Drive, Fairfield, OH 45014-5452; 513-860-1178).

The Direct Marketing Association

This trade group, founded in 1917, provides a variety of services for shoppers. It prints a catalog of mail-order houses that meet its criteria for good service (see "Sources That List Catalogs," page 16) and *Tips for Telephone Shopping*, a free booklet of guidelines for buying by phone, including information on 900 numbers, computerized calls, and consumers' rights. For a copy, write to Consumer Affairs Department, Direct Marketing Association, 6 East 43rd Street, New York, NY 10017.

The DMA can also help you if you're having trouble resolving a dispute over a mail or phone order. (Contact the Mail Order Action Line, Direct Marketing Association, 6 East 43rd Street, New York, NY 10017. Or call 212-768-7277; the number for the hearing-impaired is

212-297-1362.) And it provides services to reduce the number of solicitations you receive. The Mail Preference Service removes your name from national mailing lists that many advertisers use, and the Telephone Preference System takes your name off national phone sales lists. To register, send your full name and address and/or phone number to the Mail and/or Telephone Preference Service, Direct Marketing Association, Box 9008, Farmingdale, NY 11735-9008.

The Better Business Bureau

Contrary to what most people think, Better Business Bureaus are not government agencies but private, nonprofit organizations that promote local businesses. As part of its job, the BBB encourages members to maintain good relationships with customers. To that end, BBBs can provide some valuable aid to consumers. Here's how to use yours:

1. **Call before making a purchase.** If an ad catches your eye, but you're not familiar with the company, the BBB can give you an idea of what kind of operation it runs. But don't expect endorsements—or condemnations, for that matter. As a rule, the operator gives you only general information. If customers have complained, you'll find out whether the company was responsive, but some BBBs won't tell you what the complaints were. You'll find out whether the company has a record of deceptive advertising, but some BBBs won't tell you which products or services were promoted falsely. If an order or judgment has been filed against the company by the state attorney general or Consumer Protection Agency, the BBB will tell you and usually send you a written report if one is available. Most BBBs tell you whether the company you've called about is a member, but don't assume that all members are reputable firms. Some bad eggs slip through.

Though the BBB can be slight on specifics, ordinarily you can tell when it would be better *not* to do business with a firm, and the BBB can be especially helpful when checking out contractors, mechanics, and other service-oriented businesses.

2. **Check out charities.** If you would like to give money to a cause that seems worthy—but you're not sure—call your local BBB. Many bureaus offer reports of local and national charities. If not, they can refer you to places that do.

3. Settle disputes. If you've made a purchase and are feeling abused by unkept promises or shoddy merchandise, the BBB can often help resolve the matter. First try to settle the dispute yourself, but if that doesn't work, the mere mention of the BBB in the presence of other customers might do the trick. If the merchant still fails to comprehend the level of your dissatisfaction, a phone call or letter from the BBB frequently works. Failing that, arbitration by trained volunteers is offered by most BBBs. Owners of businesses are likely to be as eager to avoid legal expenses as you are. Many large businesses, including car manufacturers, defer to the judgment of BBB arbitrators, and some BBBs require companies to agree to arbitration as a condition of membership.

Most BBBs offer these services without charge to consumers. The Council of Better Business Bureaus in Washington, DC, also publishes pamphlets covering everything from choosing a nursing home to hiring a tax preparer. For a list, call the Council at 703-276-0100.

When You Have a Complaint

If the Better Business Bureau can't help you with your complaint, call the trade association for the business you're dealing with or contact your local or state Consumer Protection Agency. Most areas also have private consumer-advocacy groups; check in the phone book under "Consumer." John Dorfman's *Consumer Tactics Manual: How to Get Action on Your Complaints* (Atheneum) covers a variety of routes you can take to right a wrong.

□ □ □

Addendum:

Penny Pincher's Shopping Calendar

There are two rules of thumb when it comes to bargain shopping. First, buy things when you see them at a good price—not necessarily when you need them. A bathing suit might not be first on your list of priorities at the end of August, but you'll thank yourself the following June if you snap up that great red bikini at half price. Which brings us to the second rule: Shop just after the peak demand for an item. That's when retailers must move merchandise quickly to make room for new stock. Keep an eye out for sale announcements in your local paper, and keep in mind these month-by-month pointers:

January: Almost everything goes on sale in January. The trouble is that most of us are too busy paying December bills to rake in the best bargains of the year. Stock up on holiday supplies for next year at giveaway prices. Stores are also discounting the popular gift items—like bikes and toys—that arrived in huge shipments in December. Buy all-purpose gifts, such as picture frames and vases, to give throughout the year, and pick up formal clothing, dressy shoes, and fancy accessories at no-nonsense prices.

February: Stores are in a hurry to clear floor space for spring lines, so look for rock-bottom prices on remaining winter-clothing stock. Snap up a winter coat and boots, and search the bargain bins for steals on hats, scarves, and gloves. February is also sale season for leather goods and luggage.

March-April: While the spotlight is on spring and summer fashions, head over to the appliance department and invest in a new humidifier for next winter. This is the time to buy hair dryers, electric curlers, shavers, and the like. April is the best month to find rain gear on sale, from inexpensive slickers to lined trench coats.

May-June: When people start heading outside, think about shopping for inside: kitchen utensils, china, and pots and pans are all likely to be marked down. This is also the time to put in wall-to-wall carpeting or purchase a new entertainment center.

July: Now that the prom and wedding seasons are over and most people are concentrating on heading to the beach, look for deals on formalwear for men and women. Buy jewelry, too—both real and costume. Also look for major household appliances: ovens, refrigerators, washers and dryers, and dishwashers. Most of the big department-store bathing-suit sales take place this month, and many stores have concurrent lingerie and underwear sales.

August: Gear up for next summer now while everything from lawn furniture to picnic baskets is greatly reduced. Smaller stores are unloading bathing suits, sandals, sundresses, and hats. Those large decorative beach towels go on sale, too, and they make great gifts. Check out the sporting-goods stores, especially for tennis rackets, athletic shoes and apparel, and camping equipment.

September: Back-to-school fever is in the air, but the merchandise to go for is lawn and garden equipment. Replace your lawn sprinklers or riding mower, and get the buy of the year on an air conditioner or ceiling fan. If you've been thinking about putting in a swimming pool, Labor Day weekend is the time to take the plunge.

October: Those new school shoes are probably reduced by now, as are sneakers and book bags. Outerwear, from leather jackets to wool coats, is also priced to sell fast. The best coat sales take place in the first half of October, around Columbus Day. Look for good prices on appliances like sewing machines, vacuum cleaners, and power tools.

November-December: In the fierce competition for preholiday business, stores have begun offering the traditional post-Christmas sales earlier. The drawback: Stores are mobbed, lines are long, and parking spaces are few and far between. Shop as early as possible to save time for family and friends. Seek deals at health clubs (*before* those New Year's resolutions), and check out prices on cars and other major non-gift items. This is also the time to scan the classifieds for used furniture and cars, since cash-hungry sellers are likely to strike a deal favorable to you.

Chapter 2

Food

Savings in this chapter...

Many people feel that it's almost impossible to cut food costs. We have to eat, after all, and food is so much more than nourishment. It's the centerpiece of celebrations, holidays, and social get-togethers. We even use it to keep our children happy. Is it possible to do all that and cut costs at the same time?

Not only is it possible, but thriftiness and good cooking go hand in hand. Too many families spend too much money on convenience foods, fast food, and other culinary rip-offs because they think cooking at home is hard work. But with a little planning, it doesn't have to be.

The first thing you have to do is develop a renewed appreciation for food. Get in the habit of really tasting the foods you eat. When you do, simpler will seem better. Why lavish butter on that fresh ear of corn when it masks the delicate, sweet natural flavor? Do those strawberries really need to be topped with whipped cream? Not if they're ripe and juicy. Simpler foods are cheaper and usually better for you.

The second requirement is that you get organized. Once you set up an efficient kitchen (page 37), a pantry that makes cooking easy (page 40), and a food-shopping system that delivers the most for your money (below), you'll be cutting cooking costs more than you thought possible.

When you're organized, cooking from scratch instead of from a mix makes sense. Contrary to popular belief, it's just as fast, and the result costs less, tastes better, and is free of additives and artificial flavor. If you plan ahead, preparing breakfast is not a terrible task. You'll love pocketing the $350 or more a year that many people spend on doughnuts and coffee on the way to work.

In an organized kitchen, leftovers are time and money savers that you can rely on. They allow you to brown-bag lunch or heat up a quick meal after a long day of work instead of wasting your dining-out budget on so-so Chinese food. If you're creative and organized, you'll always have something to open and heat or thaw and zap.

Most important of all is that you put joy and energy back into cooking. Preparing meals shouldn't be just another chore but a caring and creative family effort performed with enthusiasm. Children can do more than set the table and load the dishwasher. Teaching your kids how to cook is a good way to spend time with them while passing down information that they'll need later.

□ □ □

A Dozen Ways to Cut Your Grocery Bill

Groceries consume a large chunk of the family budget, but you don't have to adopt a diet of beans and rice to save at the supermarket. Follow these steps and cut costs while enjoying better-tasting, more wholesome, more nutritious foods.

1. Plan ahead. Before you shop, list the items you'll need for the week ahead. Read the ingredients for any recipe you're planning to make, and look in the refrigerator, freezer, and pantry for staples that have run out. Check the newspaper to see what specials your supermarket has advertised. Shop once a week, and try not to go back to the store in between.

2. Keep your wits about you in the store. Stick to your list, but be flexible at the same time. If a recipe calls for fresh apricots, but the only ones in the store were flown in from halfway around the world and cost triple what you usually pay, can you use peaches instead? What about canned or dried apricots? Or better yet, why not postpone that dish and take advantage of the sale on strawberries?

Always read the store's weekly shopping-specials guide; search for items on your list as well as pantry staples. Save money on meat by buying large quantities when it's on sale and freezing it. And be sure to compare prices by unit (pounds, ounces, cups, and so forth). Package sizes can deceive. Most supermarket chains display unit prices, but if yours doesn't, ask the manager to begin doing so.

3. Stock up. If you have adequate storage space, save by stocking up on dry goods at a wholesale store or buying in bulk at your supermarket. Many grocery stores sell loose cereal, coffee, dried beans, flour, sugar, and spices. The prices are usually lower than if you buy those foods in packages, and because you buy only as much as you need, you avoid waste. If your grocer doesn't sell bulk foods, ask whether he'll give you a discount for quantity buys.

4. Shop alone whenever possible. Others will encourage you to stray from your budgeted items. Also, avoid shopping for groceries when you're hungry, tired, or in a hurry. Leave yourself time to coordinate your week's menu with what's available in the store, to select produce carefully, and to compare prices. Shop during off-peak hours so that you are neither rushed going through the aisles nor held up at the check-out line, where you'll be tempted to make impulse purchases on magazines, candy, and high-ticket items like disposable razors and batteries.

5. Shop smart. Be aware of techniques that supermarkets use to get you to spend. Is the milk at the back of the store? That's so you have to walk through an aisle of products to get to it. Ever wonder why the flour is always on the bottom shelf? Supermarkets place the most profitable items at eye level. Notice that fresh-baked smell when you enter? The store is hoping you'll be enticed to buy more in the bakery section, as well as everywhere else. There's nothing wrong with these techniques, but understanding them makes you a smarter consumer. Many shoppers, for instance, assume that an item is on sale if it is displayed at the end of an aisle, where specials are often set up, but that's not always the case. Store managers know that shoppers have this perception, and they often stack products there to move them quickly—without benefit of a lower price.

6. Choose your grocery store carefully. Most importantly, it should offer a good balance between price and quality. Use this checklist to evaluate other factors:

- ✔ Is the store laid out in a convenient and organized way?
- ✔ Is the frozen food frozen, canned food undented, and other food properly stored and displayed?
- ✔ Does the store provide good-quality store brands?
- ✔ Does it offer good specials and back them up with an adequate supply?
- ✔ Does the store display unit prices?
- ✔ Does it stand behind the products it sells and accept returns without a battle?
- ✔ Are the employees helpful?
- ✔ Does the store provide enough check-out lanes?
- ✔ Is there adequate parking space?
- ✔ How much time and gas will you use getting there?

You might find that you prefer one store for its high-quality meats and produce and another for its good values on canned and frozen foods. That's okay as long as making two stops doesn't take too much time. But don't drive around town looking for the best bargains on certain products.

7. Don't pay someone else to do what you can do yourself. The butcher charges extra for lean cuts of meat, but it's easy to trim the fat yourself at home. Likewise, all it takes is a sharp knife and a little know-how to cut whole chickens into parts, beef into cubes or strips, and pork sirloin into the tenderloin and the top loin. Cut up your own vegetables and wash your own salad greens, and you'll make it home with more money in your pocket. Convenience foods aren't necessarily all that convenient; if you grate your own cheese, for instance, it's fresher and cheaper. Don't be lured by loud labels that scream "diet" or "heart-healthy"; you can make your own nutritious dishes by using low-fat ingredients and a little common sense.

8. Check dates. Always check the "sell by" and "best purchased by" dates on products. Often, different shipments of a product are available on the same shelf. Unless an earlier one is on sale, choose the one with the latest date to ensure less waste at home.

9. Buy store brands. Supermarket chains make a higher profit on store brands than on famous-maker brands, so they have a vested interest in keeping you happy with their brands. Take advantage of this, and reap big savings. (See "The Name-Brand Rip-off Guide," on the next page.)

10. Beware of prepared. Buy prepared food only when the time you save is more valuable than the price you pay. If your choice is between buying a roasted chicken at the supermarket or going out to dinner at a restaurant, you'll certainly save money doing the former; and sometimes you'd simply rather not make your own baked beans, but be aware that, as always, convenience doesn't come cheaply.

11. Try to buy nonfood items elsewhere. You'll pay less for shampoo, toothpaste, and shaving cream at a drugstore, and you'll find fresher flowers at a florist.

12. Look over your receipt before you leave the store. Computer scanning machines are sometimes programmed with wrong prices, and check-out clerks have been known to make a mistake or two themselves. Be sure to double-check sale prices, as mistakes in the store's favor occur most often on these.

From Grocery-Store Managers

Watch out for downsizing. Manufacturers charge more money for their products without raising prices by putting less in the container. Just because most companies sell ground coffee in the same-size cans doesn't mean they contain the same amount of coffee. Look carefully, and you'll see that weights vary from 10 ounces to a whole pound—that's a difference of more than 50%! Look for downsizing in condensed milk, canned tuna, paper towels, and baby food, and remember to always compare unit prices.

Yellow-tag sales. Keep an eye out for yellow-tag sales—indicated not on the products but on the shelves.

Shop for pre-priced products. To promote certain items, the manufacturer marks a reduced price directly on the label, and the grocer is not allowed to increase that. Look for pre-marked prices on dishwashing liquids, detergents, and other inedible products—and sometimes on juices.

Meat-department bargains. Look for meat, fish, and poultry that have reached the "last day of sale" marked on their labels. Most often they will be discounted 50%. The catch: You must eat them that day.

The Name-Brand Rip-Off Guide

Consumers tend to choose products whose names they've heard over and over; time and again, they reach for the package with the familiar design. There's no harm in buying the same product for years—but only if you're buying it because it's the tried-and-true best option, not because the product's commercial is clever and your daughter sings its jingle.

The key to becoming an informed consumer is testing products. If the famous-label brand is better, is it so much better as to justify the higher price? If the store brand is not up to snuff, would a medium-priced lesser-known brand do the trick? Keep in mind how you plan to use the product. If you're making an applesauce cake, you can get by with the store-brand applesauce even though its texture is not quite as good. Also think about what the name-brand manufacturer did to improve the product (or justify charging more for it). Is it simply a matter of adding a little cinnamon to the applesauce? You can do that yourself.

Do you live among brand-name snobs? Many children acquire this affliction from hours of watching television. Appeal to the game-loving side of your kids by holding blind comparisons for everything from soft drinks to paper towels. Not only will your children have fun doing it, but they'll learn to scrutinize advertising claims and compare prices.

Name Brand? Think Twice

Good reasons to pick a name-brand over a store brand:	*Poor reasons to pick a name-brand over a store brand:*
✔ You like the flavor, texture, or overall quality better.	✘ Its ads say the flavor, texture, and overall quality are better.
✔ It is sturdier, thicker, or will last longer.	✘ It's strong enough to perform amazing feats that you will never use it for.
✔ Its packaging will keep it fresh longer.	✘ Its packaging is brighter and more upbeat.
✔ It's on sale for a lower price than a store brand of equal quality.	✘ It's not that much more than a store brand of equal quality.
✔ You're having a dinner party and don't have time to test the store brand.	✘ You're having a dinner party and don't want your guests to see that you use store brands.

Price Comparison of Name-Brand and Store-Brand Products

We held our own test of name brands versus store brands. For the items listed below, the store brands were all of comparable or, in some cases, superior quality to the name brands. Some supermarket chains have several levels of store brands to compete with name brands; they range from a no-frills level for basics like salt and rice to a "Select" or "Manager's Choice" level for such items as fresh pasta or fancy mustards. But even the top-level products are less expensive than well-known names. Study the chart below to see how much you can save by switching to store brands.

Item	Name-brand price	Store-brand price
Cranberry-juice cocktail, 48-ounce bottle	$ 3.19	$ 2.89
Apple juice, 64-ounce bottle	2.79	1.99
Applesauce, 15-ounce jar	1.17	.75
Yellow raisins, 15-ounce box	1.99	1.79
Dried apricots, 11-ounce box	5.21	3.99
Red kidney beans, 15-ounce can	.83	.53
Spanish olives, 10-ounce jar	4.29	2.89
Tomatoes, 28-ounce can	1.59	1.29
Tomato paste, 6-ounce can	.63	.49
Frozen corn, 10-ounce box	.89	.79
Frozen spinach, 10-ounce box	.89	.59
Fresh linguine, 12-ounce package	3.59	2.39
Rice, 10-pound bag	6.99	3.99
Whole chicken, 3 pounds	8.97	4.77
Hot-dog buns, package of 8	1.79	.79
Whole-wheat bread, 24-ounce loaf	1.99	1.69
Horseradish mustard, 9-ounce jar	2.59	1.79
Vegetable oil, 24-ounce bottle	2.35	1.49
Reduced-fat Monterey Jack cheese, 1-pound package	5.38	3.99
Cream cheese, 8-ounce package	1.69	1.19
Cottage cheese, 16-ounce container	1.99	1.59
Sour cream, 16-ounce container	1.69	1.19
Butter, 1-pound box	2.69	2.49
Evaporated milk, 12-ounce can	.85	.69
Baking soda, 16-ounce box	.75	.55
Salt, 26-ounce container	.55	.45

Item	Name-brand price	Store-brand price
Sugar, 5-pound bag	2.75	2.45
Corn flakes, 18-ounce box	2.69	1.69
Oat-bran hot cereal, 16-ounce box	2.59	1.89
Grape jelly, 12-ounce jar	1.65	1.25
Chocolate-chip pecan cookies, 14-ounce package	3.98	2.99
Black-cherry soda, six 12-ounce cans	2.99	1.78
Seltzer, 1-liter bottle	.99	.50
White vinegar, 16-ounce bottle	.75	.49
Cleanser with bleach,14-ounce container	.65	.49
Scrubber sponge	.69	.59
Aluminum foil, 200 square feet	5.59	4.59
Plastic bandages, 50 assorted	3.09	1.89
Baby powder, 14-ounce container	3.59	1.29
Total	**$99.33**	**$68.93**

The difference comes to a whopping $30.40, which means that if you switched to store brands for the items above, you'd save more than 30% on your grocery bill. And if you realized those savings each week, you would save more than $1,500 a year on groceries.

Run an Efficient Kitchen

It's easy to get the most out of the things you buy for the kitchen; just follow these money-saving tips:

Buy more than you need. Plan to have leftovers. Buy enough so that Monday night's ham becomes Tuesday night's split-pea soup, and Wednesday's macaroni turns into Thursday's pasta salad. Save time and money by making a double recipe and freezing half. When storing leftovers, always place them in the smallest containers possible. It reduces contact with air and makes them last longer.

Save those scraps. Keep a container in the freezer for storing leftover vegetables, rice, pasta, even gravy. When it's filled, thaw the contents in a pot of chicken or beef broth for a wonderful soup.

Forget the dog. Restaurants often serve too much; instead of overeating, ask for a doggie bag. You'll have the next day's lunch at no cost and with no effort.

Twice the bargain. Foods that are good for you are often easier on your pocketbook, too. Skim milk is less expensive than whole, and plain frozen vegetables are cheaper than those with butter or sauces. Try legumes for a low-cost, low-fat, high-fiber meat substitute.

Turkey tactics. Avoid buying a fresh turkey right before Thanksgiving. Buy a fresh one several months beforehand (preferably on sale) and freeze it, or buy a frozen one at holiday time. The difference in taste is slight; the difference in cost, mighty.

High steaks. For a tender, juicy steak, buy porterhouse. You'll get a filet mignon and a strip steak for a lower per-pound price than for the filet mignon alone.

Pancake supper. Breakfast food is a filling, low-cost option for a quick evening meal. Pancakes, waffles, eggs, and hot cereals are all easy to fix, and kids love them.

Inside Advice ✔

From Fresh-Market Farmers

Buy top-quality produce. The better the produce, the more of it you'll be able to use—especially if you plan on storing it for more than a day.

Buy fresh herbs and dry them. If you dry your own herbs, you'll get better flavor while beating grocery-store prices. For example, a bunch of sage containing approximately 25 sprigs costs about $1 at a farmer's market and will produce around half an ounce of dried sage, whereas a half-ounce jar of dried sage from the supermarket costs $2.39. To dry herbs, place them stems-up in a lunch-size paper bag that has been punched with holes to let air circulate. Secure the top of the bag around the stems with a piece of string.

Buy small quantities. When buying produce, shop often, and don't buy more than you need for a day or two. When fresh produce gets pushed to the back of the fridge, it's usually on its way to the garbage can.

Get the right amount. Most farmers at roadside stands or markets are happy to split a pint of cherry tomatoes or cut a watermelon in half for you. Just ask. Don't pay for something you don't want.

Educate yourself. The more you know about food, the more wisely you shop. Cookbooks like *The Fannie Farmer Cookbook* (Knopf, $24.95) and *Joy of Cooking* (Bobbs-Merrill, $9.95) are packed with valuable information on choosing, storing, cooking, and preserving produce and other foods—use them.

Thrifty snack. The next time you carve a pumpkin, don't be so fast to throw away those seeds you find inside. Instead, rinse them under cool water, pat dry, and then bake them in a 350° oven for 30 minutes or until they turn light brown. Toss the toasted seeds lightly with salted butter and a pinch of cayenne pepper.

Juicy fruit. Get more juice out of lemons, limes, and oranges by running them under hot water before squeezing them.

Table for two. You have to be especially creative to cook for just two people on a budget. For additional cost-cutting ideas, menu-planning tips, and recipes, order a copy of the U.S. Department of Agriculture's *Thrifty Meals for Two: Making Food Dollars Count.* Send a check for $2.50 to R. Woods, Consumer Information Center-2C, Box 100, Pueblo, CO 81002. Request booklet No. 115Y.

Eat More of What You Buy

One way to save on your grocery bill is to cut down on the amount of food you throw out. We all occasionally find that container of unidentifiable green fuzzy stuff in the back of the refrigerator. But for the sake of economy and health—not to mention avoiding nasty comments from family members—try to minimize the number of times that unpleasant scenario occurs. By our estimate, you can reduce waste and cut your food bill by about 10% by following these simple guidelines:

Be sure the store has taken good care of the food. Don't buy refrigerated items that aren't cold, frozen items that aren't frozen solid, or canned goods that are dented or bulging.

Thaw or marinate food in the refrigerator—not at room temperature. And never leave perishable food out of the refrigerator for more than two hours. When you're out running errands, leave your grocery shopping until the end. Once the bags are in the car, take them straight home.

Clean your refrigerator regularly to prevent cross-contamination of foods. Be especially careful with meat and poultry. Store them on plates so that their juices don't drip on other foods.

Organize your refrigerator. Designate a shelf for items that need to be used right away.

Beware of mold. If you find mold on hard cheese, salamis, or firm fruits or vegetables, you can generally salvage them by cutting off a large area around the mold, but other moldy foods should be discarded. Never taste food that has a peculiar look or smell.

Don't Toss It

Sometimes it just takes a new way of looking at things to see trash as treasure. Before you throw the following foods away, try giving them a second life:

☞ Use **sour milk** to make pancake batter.
☞ Turn **stale bread** into bread pudding.
☞ Make banana bread with **overripe bananas**.
☞ Use **dried-up pound cake** to make French toast.
☞ Crush **stale corn flakes** and use them as flour in cookie recipes.
☞ Use **old wine** to dilute wine vinegars that are too strong.

Keep a Perfect Pantry

Buy in bulk when pantry staples go on sale, and always keep plenty of dry goods around. It'll help you cut down on trips to the store and allow you to whip up a quick meal when you might otherwise go out to a restaurant or order pizza.

Your pantry should be cool, dark, and dry. To get the most out of pantry foods, it's important to know their shelf lives. For those that don't provide expiration dates, use the following recommended storage times and mark your own expiration date on the box or can. (If you store dry goods in canisters, tear off from the carton the expiration date, product code, and consumer-information phone number, and tape it to the canister.)

If you're cooking for only one or two people, larger quantities of pantry staples may not be a better buy. It takes a lot of baking to use up one of those large baking-powder cans, and you won't save any money if you end up throwing away the last third. Buy smaller amounts or consider splitting pantry items with a neighbor.

Stockpile these items that keep indefinitely:
Baking soda. To test it, pour a slight amount in your hand and add a few drops of lemon juice or vinegar; if it fizzes, it still works.
Canned fruits and vegetables*. For best flavor, color, and nutritional value, use within two years.

Canned soup*. For best flavor, use within two years.
Cocoa. Be sure container is tightly closed. Heat won't affect it, but moisture will harden it.
Cooking oil.
Cornstarch.
Corn syrup. If it shows signs of mold or fermentation, throw it out.
Dried pasta. For best flavor, use within a year.
Flour.
Jams, jellies, and preserves. For best flavor and color, use within a year.
Molasses. Be sure container is airtight.
Mustard*. For best flavor, use within a year and a half.
Salt.
Sugar (granulated, brown, or powdered). Store brown sugar in an airtight container to prevent hardening.
Vinegar. Sediment or a change in color won't affect the quality.

Stock these items only if you'll use them within the recommended storage time:
Baking chocolate: 2 years. When chocolate turns white on the outside, it is drying out.
Baking powder: 1 1/2 to 2 years. To test it, dissolve a teaspoon of baking powder in a quarter cup of hot water. If it bubbles within a few seconds, it's fine.
Canned tuna*: 3 years for water-packed, 5 years for oil-packed.
Cornmeal: 1 year. It may fade in less time if exposed to sunlight.
Dried herbs: 2 years. Old herbs won't hurt you, they just lose their flavor. To test for pungency, simply smell or taste them.
Dried beans: 1 to 1 1/2 years.
Dried fruit: 2 years.
Grits (regular and instant): 9 months to a year.
Nuts: 6 months in the pantry, 2 years in the freezer.
Oats: 1 year.
Peanut butter: 1 year.
Rice: 2 years.
Spices: 4 to 5 years for whole spices, 2 to 3 years for ground spices.
Vanilla and other extracts: 4 years.

*Unopened. (Refrigerate after opening.)
Note: Most of the items above won't hurt you if you use them after the recommended storage time, but they might be ineffective. If you're

unsure, call the manufacturer's consumer-relations department (many have toll-free numbers), for help in figuring out the product's age from the code on the package or judging whether it's still usable.

Preserving the Bounty: Canning, Freezing, and Drying Tips

It is not only economical but extremely satisfying to grow your own fruits and vegetables in the summer and preserve them for use in the winter. Even buying produce in season and preserving it will save you money. For instance, you can buy a pint of blueberries in August for about $1.49 and freeze them to use in February, but if you go to the supermarket in February (or any other month) to buy the same amount of frozen blueberries, you'll pay around $2.90.

For information about preserving food, check your cookbooks or consult these sources:

☞ For free information about canning and freezing, including how to make pickles, jams, and jellies, contact Kerr Consumer Affairs (2444 West 16th Street, Chicago, IL 60608; 312-226-1700).

☞ The U.S. Department of Agriculture publishes the latest safety information on canning. For a copy of *Complete Guide to Home Canning*, send $2.75 to the Superintendent of Documents, U.S. Government Printing Office, Washington, DC 20402. Ask for handbook No. 001-000-045229.

☞ Most libraries have lots of books on preserving foods. Two to look for: *Putting Food By* by Janet Greene, Ruth Hertzberg, and Beatrice Vaughan (The Stephen Greene Press) and *The Complete Food Preservation Book* by Beverly Barbour (David McKay Company). Both cover all aspects of canning, freezing, drying, preserving, pickling, and curing foods.

☐ ☐ ☐

How to Select a Good-Value Wine

So many varied and quirky factors go into making a wine expensive—from a nation's foreign-exchange rates to a wine-maker's runaway ego—that value in fine wine can be a tough thing to judge. Some wines are simply so rare or coveted that $100 a bottle is considered a bargain by experts. Some wines aren't worth a hoot at any price. The most important factor is your own taste. Many people like slightly sweet wines; others can't stand anything but the driest of the dry. Some like bubbly wines that give others a headache just to contemplate. No matter what you've heard, there is no standard taste or guide. The best way to find bargains is to try new wines and remember—or better yet, write down—what you like. Your taste is the only taste that counts. Some suggestions for where to start:

A Dozen Great White Wines Under $10

Domestic:
De Loach Gewürztraminer, "Early Harvest"
Robert Mondavi, Napa Valley Fumé Blanc
Vichon "Chevrignon"
Buena Vista Sauvignon Blanc
Preston Vineyards "Cuvée de Fume"
Benziger Pinot Blanc
Meridian Chardonnay
Villa Mt. Eden Chardonnay

Imported:
Moreau et Fils Macon-Villages (France)
Barton & Guestier (B&G) Chardonnay (France)
Rosemount Estate Chardonnay (Australia)
Lindeman's "Bin 65" Chardonnay (Australia)

A Dozen Great Red Wines Under $10

Domestic:
Bonny Doon, "Grahm Crew"
Chateau Souverain Zinfandel
Ravenswood Zinfandel, "Vintner's Blend"
Estancia Cabernet Sauvignon
Columbia Crest Merlot

Imported:
Jabôulet "Parallele 45" Côtes du Rhone (France)
Guigal Côtes du Rhone (France)
Penfolds "Koonunga Hill" (Australia)
Georges Duboeuf Beaujolais-Villages (France)
Michel Lynch Bordeaux (France)
Marques de Arienzo Rioja (Spain)
Antinori Santa Cristina (Italy)

Top five generic "jug" wines. When you're looking for some cost-effective wines to serve at a picnic or other large gathering, don't snub those ungainly oversize bottles you see at stores. For the right occasion, the taste and price fit. Try the jug wines of these wine-makers: Taylor California Cellars, Gallo, Paul Masson, Los Hermanos, Inglenook Navalle.

The best deal around. Chilean Cabernet Sauvignons, priced between $5 and $9, offer some of the best red wine bargains. Try the reds of: Errazuriz, Los Vascos, Caliterra, Miguel Torres, Santa Rita, Concha y Toro, or (for a little more, and worth it) Cousino Macul.

Kitchenware Bargains

While great cooks have been known to whip up fantastic meals seemingly out of thin air, over the long haul any successful kitchen must be well-equipped. There are certain things a serious cook must have. They include a large stove/oven (preferably gas), a big refrigerator with a separate freezer, a deep sink (or better, two), plenty of cabinets and counter space, an assortment of sturdy pots and pans, a set of good-quality knives, a variety of utensils, and some basic small appliances—a toaster, a blender, a hand-held mixer, and probably a microwave.

These are the essentials. And then there are the products that depend on your preferences. Most people drink coffee every morning, so they buy an electric coffee maker; that makes sense. But if you'd only make ice cream on the Fourth of July, you might not want to invest in an electric ice-cream machine. If you eat cereal every morning, a waffle maker is just going to collect dust. And if you don't do a lot of chopping, you probably don't need a food processor in addition to your blender.

Most of us have gotten used to the ease of electric appliances, but often the manual version is just as easy to use, less expensive to buy and operate, and more dependable. Think before you buy. You can't beat manual can openers, juicers, or knife sharpeners. When a recipe calls for tools you don't have, see if you can make do with something you already own. Start with these suggestions:

Instead of buying...	Try using...
a biscuit cutter	a glass
a cake rack	a roasting-pan rack
a double boiler	a metal bowl over a saucepan
an electric steamer	a steamer basket in a saucepan
a food processor	a food mill
an ice-cream scoop	a spoon run under hot water
a kettle	a covered saucepan
a meat pounder	a hammer
a pastry blender	two knives
a pizza cutter	kitchen scissors
a sifter	a sieve and a spoon
a trussing needle	a needlepoint needle
a zester	the small side of a grater

Shopping for kitchenware. Compare prices from stores around town with those from these top mail-order wholesalers. Write or call for free catalogs:

☞ Colonial Garden Kitchens, Hanover, PA 17333-0066; 717-633-3333.

☞ Kitchen Etc., 31 Lafayette Road, Box 1560, North Hampton, NH 03862; 800-232-4070.

☞ Robin Importers, Inc., 510 Madison Avenue, New York, NY 10022; 212-753-6475. Send self-addressed, stamped business-size envelope for list of brands.

□ □ □

Saving Energy in the Kitchen

It takes a lot of electricity to run a busy kitchen. For instance, your refrigerator can account for as much as a third of your electricity bill. Refrigerators are the only major appliances that run 24 hours a day, 365 days a year. But ovens and stoves also eat up a lot of energy. The following tips will help you use your appliances without burning money.

Cool Your Refrigerator Costs

Clean the coils. At least twice a year, unplug your refrigerator and dust and vacuum the exposed coils in the back.

Regulate the temperature. A refrigerator that is too cold wastes energy. Your refrigerator should be kept at 40°F, and your freezer at 0°F.

Keep your freezer as full as possible. That way when you open and close it, less warm air, which must be cooled, will be captured there. Take advantage of meat or frozen juice specials at your grocery store. If you don't have food to freeze, make some ice and store it in bags in your freezer.

Free zone. Your refrigerator, on the other hand, should not be packed so full that air cannot circulate around the food.

Make sure door seals are tight. Test them by closing the door over a dollar bill. If you can pull the bill out easily, the latch needs adjusting or the seal replacing.

Cover liquids. Otherwise they make the refrigerator air more humid and harder to cool. Allow hot foods to cool somewhat before refrigerating them.

Consider trading in your old refrigerator. Newer, more energy-efficient models use about a third less electricity than models built more than a decade ago, which translates into approximate savings of $30 to $45 a year (see page 72).

Save a Trove at Your Stove

Hot water. Boil only as much water as you need. Use a kettle or a covered pan, and turn the burner off as soon as the water reaches a boil.

Pots and pans. To prevent wasted heat, match pot and pan sizes as closely as possible to burner sizes. Flat bottoms conduct heat more efficiently than rounded bottoms. Use lids whenever possible. Foods cook fastest when covered.

Don't be a gusher. If you use a gas range, check to see that your flame is blue and cone-shaped. Keep burners clean for best results, and don't let the flame reach the pot or pan. The maximum heat is just above the flame's tip.

Buying a gas stove. When it's time to replace old appliances, shop for a gas oven or range with an automatic (electronic) ignition system instead of pilot lights. You'll save an average of up to 40% in the oven and 50% on the stove top.

Operate Your Oven Efficiently

Turn it on at the right time. It's not always necessary to preheat. Baked goods and dishes with a cooking time of less than an hour require a preheated oven. For everything else, turn the oven on when you place the dish inside. When you do need to preheat the oven, five minutes will do.

Lower the heat. If you use glass or ceramic baking dishes, which retain heat better than metal, you can lower the temperature of your oven by 25°.

Piggyback. If you're making several casseroles or other dishes that don't require exactitude, cook them all at once. Your oven uses roughly the same amount of energy no matter how many dishes are in it. If three recipes call for three different temperatures, say 325°, 350°, and 375°, set the temperature in the middle (in this case at 350°) and compensate by adjusting the cooking times.

Keep it closed. While cooking, don't open the oven door any more than necessary. The better you know your oven, the better you'll be at judging how accurate recipe cooking times are for you.

Turn it off early. Turn off the oven several minutes before the dish is done. Let the retained heat finish the cooking.

Clean it with care. Keep your oven clean for maximum efficiency. Mix white vinegar and water to make an inexpensive but effective oven cleaner. If your electric oven is a self-cleaner, the most efficient time to clean it is immediately after cooking while it's still hot.

□ □ □

— Chapter 3 —

The Home

Savings in this chapter...

In addition to being the single biggest investment you'll probably ever make, your home also requires the costliest upkeep of anything you own. In fact, according to the U.S. Bureau of Labor Statistics, the average family forks over $2,650 a year on routine cleaning, minor repairs, and supplies alone. Some people might call this a burden, but good penny pinchers know an opportunity when they see one.

You can start by swapping the dozen or so specialty cleaning products beneath your kitchen sink for a bottle of white vinegar. For around a dollar, vinegar and a little elbow grease will fill most of your cleaning needs. And what vinegar won't do, borax probably will. If not,

chances are we've got another substitute. For example, all you need to clean a grease stain from your carpet is a little baking soda or cornstarch (see page 52), two inexpensive household staples you probably keep handy anyway.

Whether you're trying to start and maintain that green lawn you always wanted (page 54), dealing with pests in a way that won't contaminate your home (page 53), breathing new life into that expensive rug (page 52), or picking out chairs for the room you're redecorating, there are ways to to cut costs. And when you're faced with minor repairs, rather than hiring someone, do the job yourself. Fix a leaky faucet (page 58) or patch a window screen (page 55). It requires little skill, hardly any time, and you'll enjoy the feeling of accomplishment. When you do need to hire a professional repairman or an interior designer to help you really spruce up, see our tips for how to avoid paying too much (page 59).

□ □ □

Saving Big on Household Chores

Every day, you're faced with household chores—scrubbing bathroom, washing clothes, maintaining the lawn. The bright side is that cutting costs on these, you can save money just as regularly. To the chores more meaningful, involve the kids, but don't just send out into the yard alone. Designate a few hours when everybod together. Getting them to lend a hand not only saves you money but also teaches them the value and fun of teamwork.

Housework Hints

Remembering twice-a-year chores. A good twice-a-year chores, like turning mattresses, rugs, an makes them last longer, is when you change the clo daylight saving time and back again.

Sharpening scissors. Cut through fine scissors. This also works for sewing machine the paper a few times.

Preventing wicker wear. Prolong th vacuuming every month or so. And for al wicker, use a spritzer bottle filled with wat

twice a year (but no more).

Conserving candles. Make candles burn slower by placing them in the freezer for several hours before lighting them.

Cleaning on the Cheap

Cleaning a dirty microwave. To clean a microwave oven, boil a bowl of water in it for a few minutes. The steam will loosen the stuck-on food. Then you can wipe the inside clean with a soapy sponge or rag.

Cleaning floors and walls. Add half a cup of borax, half a teaspoon of dishwashing liquid, and a tablespoon of ammonia to two gallons of warm water for a cheap alternative to commercial wall and floor cleaners.

Deodorizing the toilet. To deodorize your toilet bowl, sprinkle in a quarter cup of borax, swish around with a toilet brush and let it stand overnight.

Removing vinyl floor rust. Bleach removes rust stains from vinyl floor tiling in your kitchen. To make sure the bleach won't alter the color of the tiles, test it in an inconspicuous area.

Getting rid of crayon marks. Remove crayon marks from walls by scrubbing with a paste of baking soda and water.

Reusing sponges. Get more mileage out of your sponges by putting them through the dishwasher, on the top rack. If you use six sponges an extra six months each, you'll save about $2.50—and help the environment.

Cleaning with vinegar. For hundreds of years, vinegar has been a cooking necessity. But this workhorse is also a must around any thrifty household for a variety of cleaning projects:

$$ Price Comparison: Vinegar vs. Commercial Products $$	
Vinegar (16 oz.):	75¢ (name brand), 49¢ (store brand)
Window cleaner (16 oz.):	$1.96 (name brand)
Bathtub cleaner (16 oz.):	$2.25 (name brand)

Removing tough stains from china. An equal mixture of vinegar and salt cleans tough coffee and tea stains from china cups.

Cleaning fish tanks. A safe way to clean your aquarium is a rag doused in white vinegar. Be sure to rinse thoroughly.

☞ **Scrubbing the tub.** Use vinegar to remove the film that builds up in the bathtub. Rinse the tub clean with water.

☞ **Peeling away decals.** When you're tired of old window decals, paint them thoroughly with a coat of vinegar. Let them soak for several minutes, then wipe them off with ease.

☞ **Cleaning copper pots.** Use salt, vinegar, and a little elbow grease to clean copper pots.

☞ **Washing windows.** Clean windows with a half-and-half mixture of warm water and vinegar, and you won't have to worry about leaving an unsightly film or streaking. Dry with a soft cloth or, even better, crumpled-up newspaper.

Think Twice Before You Toss

A great way to save money around the house is to recycle. If you're resourceful, you can find a second life for many used products or spent containers. And if you do, you can feel good about helping the environment, too.

Old toothbrushes. Save old toothbrushes to clean hard-to-reach places in the kitchen and tile grout in the bathroom.

Vacuum-cleaner bags. Some vacuum-cleaner bags can be recycled. Just cut off the bottom to empty and then reseal by stapling.

Foil pie plates. Cut one of these in half for a ready-made dustpan.

Old window screens. When you need a heavy-duty sanding block for scraping paint from wood, wrap a piece of screen around a wood block. It works wonders without damaging the wood.

Three uses for eggshells. 1. If you have a dirty vase with a small opening, drop in a couple of crushed shells along with water and vinegar or detergent. Cover the mouth of the vase and shake it until it's clean. Empty the mixture and rinse. **2.** Mix crushed eggshells into potting soil. They contain many nutrients that plants need. **3.** Poke a drainage hole in the bottom of several shell halves. Fill them with soil and seedlings, and store them in an egg carton until planting time. Then crack the shells and plant them with the sprouts. They will decompose and provide minerals.

Peach pits and fruit stones. Dry them out and save them in a jar. The next time you have a fire in the fireplace, throw a couple on. They'll crackle and pop while emitting a pleasant fruity smell.

How to Make Your Carpets Live Longer

Of all the things that fill your house, your carpets get the least respect. They are constantly trampled upon by hordes of dirty feet. Odors cling to them. Children spill food and drinks on them. And the family pets call them home.

But carpets are expensive and meant to last. With the right care and cleaning, they will. For quick answers to questions about do-it-yourself or professional carpet cleaning, call the Dupont hotline at 800-4DUPONT. You can also request a copy of Dupont's *Complete Book of Carpeting*. If you give your carpet the TLC it deserves and follow these suggestions, you might never have to buy another:

Use doormats. Place a doormat at each outside entrance and encourage all family members to make a habit of using them in fair weather and foul.

Clean regularly. Don't let dirt build up in your carpet. Vacuum rugs and carpets thoroughly once a week, and high-traffic areas more often, especially when soil is noticeable. Use a mixture of one cup of vinegar per gallon of water on dirty spots and then blot dry.

Reduce fading. Keep direct sunlight off rugs and carpet as much as is practical. Shades, blinds, draperies, shutters, and awnings help. When possible, place rugs away from windows.

Attend to spills immediately. Use a modest amount of neutral detergent and a damp colorless cloth to wipe stains clean. Be sure not to wet the carpet excessively.

Remove stains. For really tough stains, like red wine or grape juice, first blot up any liquid. Soak the stained area with a cloth dipped in a mixture of water, 5% hydrogen peroxide, and 5% household ammonia. Blot again, rinse with clean water, then blot once more. Next, rub the area with a laundry stain remover. Blot the excess, rinse with water, then blot dry. Weigh down four or five layers of paper towels on the spot for five to 10 minutes. Repeat this step until no stain appears on towels. Let carpet dry completely, then vacuum.

For grease stains. Rub grease lightly with baking soda, or cover it with cornstarch. After an hour, vacuum or brush the carpet clean.

Mud. Let mud dry, then vacuum. Sponge it clean with dishwashing liquid.

Steam-clean occasionally. Professional hot-water extraction cleaning ensures the health of your carpets better than home shampooing. Save money by renting a steam cleaner and doing it yourself. Use the yellow pages to shop for the best deal.

Save scraps. Save a section of new carpet in case disaster strikes. For burns and other permanent damage, use a razor knife to cut out a square that encompasses the ruined section. Place the ruined square on the saved section and cut out an identical piece. Use double-faced tape to secure the new section in the hole.

Renew colors. Mix one cup of white vinegar with a gallon of water; brush into rugs or carpets to restore natural colors.

□ □ □

Low-Cost Pest Control (That's Environmentally Correct)

As with household cleaning, the world of pest control is teeming with expensive specialty products—insect sprays, flea powders, pellets, traps, and even motels for cockroaches. The American Kennel Club estimates that each year, dog owners spend, on average, $80 per dog for flea and pest treatment. What a lot of families don't know is that with a few inexpensive household staples, they've already got what it takes to kill most pests.

Ants. To deter ants, wash countertops, cabinets, and floors with equal parts of vinegar and water.

Fleas. Add a teaspoon of vinegar to each quart bowl of drinking water that you give to your pets to help keep them free of ticks and fleas. (The ratio of one teaspoon to one quart is for a 40-pound animal; use less for smaller animals.) To kill fleas, score the skin of an orange and rub the juice directly into your pet's coat. Be sure not to get juice in his eyes. Vacuum frequently around your pet's favorite resting spots, and place eucalyptus branches there. Sprinkle table salt lightly around the same areas.

Mosquitoes. Conventional insect repellents do work, but in addition to being costly, they contain "DEET," which is under investigation for safety by the EPA. Citronella oil, which is inexpensive and available in most hardware stores, has been used for decades as a natural repellent. Or try rubbing a little apple-cider vinegar on your skin. If mosquitoes are a problem inside, use a yellow light bulb outside to attract them there. Leave an open bottle of pennyroyal or citronella oil in your room.

Cockroaches. To kill roaches, add half a cup of flour and a quarter cup of sugar to a cup of borax and sprinkle along cracks and crevices where they hide. Another deterrent: Mix lime juice, water, crushed bay leaves, and a small amount of table salt together. Apply to infested areas.

Silverfish. Sprinkle cinnamon into cupboards and drawers and onto bookshelves to get rid of these pests.

▫ ▫ ▫

Lawn Care For Less: Ten Steps

The smart homeowner can have grass without spending too much green. To start a lawn, you should seed rather than sod. The average cost to lay sod is 25 cents per square foot, about $2,500 for a 10,000-square-foot area. A 50-pound bag of improved fescue seed, on the other hand, which also covers 10,000 square feet, costs only about $90. Remember that grass doesn't grow well in dense shade. Instead, plant alternatives like ferns, ivy, or hostas under trees.

1. Do your homework. Select the type of grass recommended for your area. Talk to your agricultural extension agent before making the final decision if there is any doubt.

2. Time it right. When seeding a lawn, timing is crucial. Some turf types germinate best in cool weather while others need soil temperatures of 60°F or higher. Some need to be covered in order to germinate; others need to be exposed to filtered light. Read the label before you buy.

3. Don't fertilize at the same time you seed. This wastes money because much of the food value of the fertilizer has leached out by the time the seed has germinated and developed a root system capable of absorbing nutrients.

4. Don't overfertilize. Not only does this waste money, but it increases the amount of mowing required and encourages lush growth that falls prey to insects and disease. Be sure to follow the instructions on the fertilizer package.

5. Don't underfeed either. To grow well, grass needs a steady diet of nutrients. Hungry plants are less resistant to insects and disease. If you're in doubt about the proper amount, ask for advice at your garden-supply store.

6. Use slow-nitrogen-release fertilizer. Also called organic or insoluble nitrogen, this type of fertilizer is more expensive but lasts for months rather than days or weeks like some "budget" formulas.

7. Water deeply. Rather than giving your lawn a quick shower every day, water deeply a couple times a week. This encourages deep, healthy roots that can better survive drought, winter weather, and weeds.

8. Weed by hand. Don't turn to weed killers every time you spot a weed. Instead, weed by hand. Get your kids to help.

9. Use a push mower. If you have a small yard (less than an eighth of an acre), use a push mower rather than a gas-powered rotary. A pushmower costs about $150 less and uses no gasoline.

10. Sharpen your mower blade. You'll use less gas with a sharp blade. And a cleaner cut, which allows grass to heal more quickly, helps prevent fungus diseases. Keep grass at least three inches long so that it shades the ground and keeps weeds from flourishing.

□ □ □

Cutting Costs on Improvements, Repairs, and Maintenance

These days, house calls by electricians, plumbers, carpenters, and painters usually cost you $50 before the work is even begun. So it pays to be able to recognize and repair the easy jobs. Often the fix is as simple as unclogging a drain or the improvement as basic as repainting the kitchen cabinets. You don't need an "expert." With the right tools and a guidebook (or a little help from a friend in the know), you'll save a bundle by tackling simple home repairs and improvements yourself.

Prevention First

Of course, the best way to avoid having to repair is to prevent damage by catching problems early. Give your home a checkup each spring. Here's what to look for:

Missing shingles and other roof problems. Catch these before water damage creates a much bigger problem inside the house.

Gutters and downspouts. Make sure water channeled from gutters washes away from the house, not toward the basement.

Paint problems. Check for peeling or bubbling paint.

Screens. Avoid the cost of replacing screens in doors and windows by mending holes. Use clear rubber cement for smaller holes and a patch kit ($2 for five or more patches) for larger tears.

Signs of termites. Check carefully for termites, searching for clues like discarded wings, piles of sawdust, or porous wood, in your home's foundation, porches, firewood, and other wood areas. Killing these destructive pests now saves you thousands of dollars in removal and repair costs later.

Be informed. When problems do arise, or when you're ready to make a home improvement, like building a deck, adding a skylight, or remodeling a bathroom, do your homework. At the local library, look for home-repair magazines like *The Family Handyman* and books such as the *Reader's Digest New Complete Do-It-Yourself Manual* and Time-Life's *Home Repair and Improvement* series. Or talk to a hardware dealer who is willing to answer your questions and add suggestions.

Save on tools. Don't spend a fortune gearing up; shop for discount tools by mail. Write or call for the Tools on Sale catalog (with 408 pages of name-brand tools!) from Seven Corners Ace Hardware, Inc. (216 West Seventh Street, St. Paul, MN 55102; 800-328-0457).

Painting Like the Pros

Painting is one of the easier and more rewarding do-it-yourself improvements. With a little know-how, you can take on walls, furniture, cabinets, even exterior surfaces, and save big. Research your equipment and paint needs, and before you lay the first coat, make sure the surface is clean, smooth, and ready to paint. For help with prep work, consult the government booklet *Stripping Paint From Wood*. Send a check for $1 (made out to Superintendent of Documents), to S. James, Consumer Information Center-2C, Box 100, Pueblo, CO 81002. Ask for item No. 571Y.

Think before you paint. When your home appears in need of a new paint job, wash it with mild detergent instead. If you can extend the lifetime of the present paint, you'll save a considerable sum.

Pay less for paint. Few things irritate the home handyman (or woman) more than being charged double the price that a contractor pays at a paint store. Although you won't be able to get a commercial discount, once you decide on your paint, shop at a warehouse-type home store, like Home Quarters Warehouse or The Home Depot. Home Quarters will even beat by 10% any lower price you find.

Sandpaper. Keep sandpaper from cracking and lengthen its life by dampening the backing.

Conserve paint. Protect and preserve paint by pouring only what you need into a bucket and working out of it instead of the paint can. Stretch a strong rubber band around the bucket lengthwise to wipe your brush on. This saves paint and keeps the bucket's edges clean.

Keep paint and brushes fresh between jobs. Add four tablespoons of mineral spirits to the top layer of oil-based paint to keep it fresh. Mix it in before the next paint job. When using oil-based paint, to maintain brushes during short breaks, wrap them in airtight plastic wrap.

Working with a pro. If you decide to hire a professional to paint or hang wallpaper, negotiate a lower cost by moving furniture, removing fixtures, and sanding yourself. Be sure to specify who will do what in your contract.

Taking Care of Basic Repairs

Besides painting and plumbing, you should be able to manage some other minor repairs yourself. Most require no special tools. For advice, call your local hardware store or pick up a how-to manual at your library. The U.S. government booklet *Simple Home Repairs* gives step-by-step instructions for some basic jobs, including repairing or replacing electric plugs, setting tile, repairing screens, replacing broken windows, and fixing problem doors. It also includes a section on using basic tools. For a copy, send a check for $1.50 (made out to Superintendent of Documents), to R. Woods, Consumer Information Center, Box 100, Pueblo, CO 81002. Ask for item No. 125Y.

Remodeling the Right Way

Sometimes it pays to make a major addition to your home—when you're considering buying a new house because you're tired of the present one, for instance. In this case, adding a deck or converting the garage into a playroom might be the answer. If so, you'll probably need to hire a contractor. These tips might help:

Inside Advice ✓

From a Plumber

Of all repairmen, the plumber is the most frequently called, for one simple reason: No one wants to mess with drains and toilets. From afar, all those parts seem mysterious and technical, and most people are terrified of what lurks in a clogged sink trap. To avoid the high cost of a house call, though, you've got to overcome this phobia. The next time a problem arises, don't reach for the phone unless you're calling a hardware dealer for advice (a good idea, by the way). Try these hints to solve your problem:

1. Preventing clogs. Reduce the threat of a clog by cleaning drains periodically and after heavy cooking. But don't use expensive and dangerous drain acids. Try a mixture of baking soda and vinegar. Drop a handful of baking soda down the drain, then pour half a cup of white vinegar on top. Cover tightly for 30 seconds, then flush with cold water.

2. The fine art of plunging. If you do experience a clogged drain, first reach for the plunger—they don't call it the plumber's helper for nothing. For best results, fill the clogged sink half full of water, making sure you cover any overflow holes. Then cover the drain with the plunger, tilt the cup to get rid of trapped air, pump up and down vigorously 10 or 15 times, and remove abruptly. Repeat until the drain is clear of debris.

3. Fixing a leaky faucet. This is one of the simple repairs you can make yourself, and all you need is a screwdriver, an adjustable wrench, and a box of assorted washers. After turning off the water at the shut-off valve, loosen the packing nut on top of the handle and remove the handle. Remove the screw holding the old washer at the bottom of the valve unit, and replace the washer with a new one.

4. Caulking a bathtub. Caulk a tub yourself using a caulking gun (about $5) and tubes of silicone sealant ($4 to $6 per tube). Place masking tape on the wall and tub to ensure a clean edge. Before caulking, fill the tub with water so that its weight will open the crack as far as possible.

5. When the toilet won't flush. Don't panic! More than likely, the problem is a broken upper lift wire, the wire that connects the lift arm to the tank ball. And the repair is easy. For less than a dollar, you can buy a foot of chain and a clasp at a hardware store and reconnect the two parts.

Shop around. Look for contractors with good references, and ask three or four for estimates, making sure you compare apples to apples (in other words, make sure each bid is, say, all-inclusive, or for labor only). When you think you've found your man, go check his work in person and talk to the customer.

Learn about contracts. The only way to protect yourself against unexpected problems such as project delays, cost overruns, and disputes is to spell out the details in a contract. Decide on a fixed-price or a time-and-materials contract and state what you'll pay up front and after the job is completed. For $5.95 (plus $1 shipping and handling), the American Homeowners Foundation (1724 South Quincy Street, Arlington, VA 22204) will provide a model agreement that you can use as a reference.

Free information. Before you hire anyone, call the National Association of Home Builders bookstore (800-223-2665) for a free copy of *How to Choose a Remodeler Who's on the Level*.

□ □ □

Elegant and Affordable Home Decorating

By making smart changes and additions, you can give new life to a room without investing a lot. Before you spend a dime, try rearranging the furniture and artwork you already own. Sometimes moving things around is all it takes to add new life. If more drastic measures are needed, browse through home-decorating magazines and books at your library for ideas. Check out do-it-yourself guides. Consider hiring an interior-design student to help. A student won't have the same experience as a professional, but then again, he or she won't charge as much either. Post a sign at local design schools or at colleges with design departments.

If you feel a project is big enough to warrant a professional designer, find one you trust. Look for someone who charges a set fee plus a reasonable commission—say, 10%—on top of furniture. Order a copy of *Hiring an Interior Designer: Explore the Possibilities* ($1), which explains the costs involved, from the American Society of Interior Designers (608 Massachusetts Avenue, NE, Washington, DC 20002). On request, ASID also recommends interior designers in your area.

Where to Find Great Budget Decorating Ideas

Check the classified advertising section in the back of home-decorating magazines for inexpensive sources for fabric, wallpaper, and other decorating materials. Women's magazines and major sewing-pattern companies also publish do-it-yourself home-decorating manuals. For more low-cost decorating ideas, look for guides in your library. A few to try: *Champagne Decorating on a Beer Budget* by Doreen Roy (Stein and Day), *The Low-Cost Guide to Designing Your Living Space* by Gerry Cooper (Arco Publishing), and *Don't Move—Improve!* by Katie and Gene Hamilton (H. Holt).

Finishing Floors on the Cheap

When it comes to floors, be creative. There are a number of low-cost, attractive alternatives to traditional rugs:

Rugs and carpets. Place a small Oriental rug—at a place of maximum visibility—on top of a room-size carpet. You get the style of the one and the durability of the other. Rag, hooked, braided, and other types of rugs can be made at home. Use old clothes, leftover paint, and other scraps. Look for how-to manuals at your library.

Pick up a free copy of *Tips on Carpet and Rugs*, a guide to selecting the appropriate floor covering, at your local Better Business Bureau. Or request a copy from the Council of Better Business Bureaus (4200 Wilson Boulevard, Suite 800, Arlington, VA 22203, Attention: Publications Department). Include a check for $1 to cover postage. For wholesale savings via mail order, request catalogs from Bearden Brothers Carpet Corporation (3200-A Dug Gap Road, Dalton, GA 30720; 800-433-0074) or Johnson's Carpets (3239 South Dixie Highway, Dalton, GA 30720; 800-235-1079).

Sensible sisal. Sisal matting is a low-cost and stylish alternative to a rug. You can even paint it to give it your own flair. Sisal with durable latex backing is available from rug and carpet dealers. Or contact Abbey Carpet (3100 Geary Boulevard, San Francisco, CA 94118; 415-752-6620) for samples and price estimates.

Canvas for an inexpensive modern look. Buy a piece of canvas two inches longer and wider than the size of the rug you want. Cut out a square inch from each corner, and fold and glue the flap on each side to the back of the canvas (they'll overlap). Prime both sides of the canvas with gesso. Now paint the rug. Copy the design from a book on Amish quilts, a piece of wrapping paper, or another rug—or make up your own. After the paint dries, seal it with a coat of polyurethane. You can make floor cloths in any size—from door mats to room-size carpets. For discount art supplies, request a free catalog from Art Express (Box 21662, Columbia, SC 29210; 800-535-5908).

Walls That Aren't Pricey

The most cost-effective way to enliven a room is with a fresh coat of paint. For a coordinated, thoughtful look, choose a light tone of the room's theme color. Gather paint chips and tape them to the wall for a few days to help you decide. *Important:* Hues are more intense when spread over a large area; be conservative.

You can create the look of expensive wallpaper by making textured wall surfaces yourself. Use leftover paints and buy stenciling patterns and sponging tools at craft or paint stores. For instructions, check at your library for a copy of Alex Davidson's *Interior Affairs: The Decorative Arts in Paintwork* (Ward Lock). It covers oil and water glazing techniques, stenciling, decoupage, marbling, bambooing, and more.

For a free copy of *How to Hang Wall Coverings*, write the National Decorating Products Association, 1050 North Lindbergh Boulevard, St. Louis, MO 63132.

Order discount catalogs for wallpaper, fabric, and window blinds from Custom Windows & Walls (32525 Stephenson Highway, Madison Heights; MI 48071; 800-772-1947), American Blind and Wallpaper Factory (28237 Orchard Lake Road, Farmington Hills, MI 48334; 800-735-5300), or Silver Wallcovering (3001-15 Kensington Avenue, Philadelphia, PA 19134; 800-426-6600).

Remaking Your Windows for Less

It's not difficult to make inexpensive gathered valances, cornices, and shades from fabric remnants with the help of how-to manuals available in libraries. Use found objects to make unusual tiebacks for curtains: In a child's room, attach cords to small teddy bears or other toys; in the living room, use fabric scraps left over from upholstering a chair; in a sewing room, use a tape measure. Bamboo poles make pretty curtain rods that are much cheaper than traditional rods. Or use large wooden dowels and paint them to match the curtains or walls.

Furniture That Fits Your Budget

Once you've decided you need new furniture, search books and magazines to find the look you want. Books like Jean Taylor Federico's *Clues to American Furniture* (Starrhill Press, $7.95) help you begin to learn styles and see bargains. The more you know about whether you want antiques, reproductions, or contemporary styles, the better prepared you are for saving money. Visit furniture stores in your area. When you decide what brands and designs you like, order a wholesale catalog or price list from Barnes & Barnes Fine Furniture (190 Commerce Avenue, Southern Pines, NC 28387; 800-334-8174), The

---

Furniture Factory Outlets

Furniture goes in and out of style frequently. When collections go out, manufacturers discontinue and unload them to make room for newer, more fashionable designs. That's where outlet stores come in.

Almost all large furniture manufacturers, most of which are located in North Carolina and Virginia, have outlet warehouses where newly obsolete furniture sells at discounted prices. If you're about to make a major furniture buy, consider a trip to the Hickory Furniture Mart (2220 Highway 70 Southeast, Hickory, NC 28602; 800-462-6278), where you'll find a dozen acres of discontinued furniture from 60 manufacturers, including Broyhill, Drexel, Bernhardt, Century, and Henredon, at prices 30% to 70% below retail. Shoppers also receive a 15% discount at three local hotels. (Ask the mart organizers when you call for information.)

Or try the High Point Atrium Furniture Mall (430 South Main Street, High Point, NC 27260; 919-882-5599), which offers four floors (225,000 square feet!) of furniture from manufacturers such as Hickory White, Baker, Pennsylvania House, and Jamestown Sterling at prices 30% to 50% below retail.

Look for outlets in the hometowns of other furniture manufacturers. For example, Bassett Furniture offers amazing bargains on discontinued collections, scratch-and-dent furniture, and showroom samples at an outlet near its factory in Virginia (Box 626, Main Street, Bassett, VA 24055; 703-629-6446). If you are interested in a particular manufacturer, call them and ask about their outlet store.

Furniture Barn (1190 Highway 74 Bypass, Spindale, NC 28160; 704-287-7106), or Loftin-Black Furniture Company (111 Sedgehill Drive, Thomasville, NC 27360; 800-334-7398).

Inside Advice ✓

From an Interior Designer

Make use of slipcovers. These low-cost alternatives to upholstery make a big impact on a room. Because they are washable, slipcovers are especially practical for families with small children. If you sew, make your own simple slipcovers that tie at the legs. Most pattern companies have easy-to-follow instructions. Order fabric wholesale from The Fabric Center (485 Electric Avenue, Fitchburg, MA 01420; 508-343-4402).

Fashion your own end tables. For an inexpensive end table, make a plywood base and cover it with a tablecloth—or even an old quilt. For an up-to-date look, use a cloth that's too long for the table and arrange the bottom in a flowing pouf. The table will be more functional if you top it with glass cut to fit by a local glazier.

Create a coffee table. Make coffee tables from found objects, like porcelain garden stools, wrought-iron stands or log holders, old wooden boxes and trunks, concrete garden ornaments, or wooden architectural elements, which you can find at junkyards.

When Antiques Are the Answer

Most people think antiques are more expensive than modern reproductions. But that isn't always the case. Certain furniture, silver, and ceramics cost more as reproductions. For example, mid-19th-century English and American chests of drawers still sell for several hundred rather than several thousand dollars, the price you'll pay for copies. Here are other antiques that are often bargains:

Chests, sideboards, and huntboards. One-hundred- to 150-year-old chests, sideboards, and huntboards with beautiful veneers are still out there. Even with replaced feet and brasses on the drawers, they feel old and provide an antique accent in a room.

Sterling-silver flatware. Antique sterling-silver flatware currently sells at prices comparable to those of new pieces by Gorham, Steiff, and others. The older pieces are generally heavier and already have a collector's value.

China. Modern European porcelains like Heren and Royal

Copenhagen are often more expensive than antique English ironstone china. Not only are the older wares historic, but they have doubled in value in the last five years alone.

Note: Many decorators recommend mixing antiques and reproductions for those trying to stay within a budget. A newly made reproduction Sheraton-style dining-room table on pedestal legs is much cheaper and easier to locate than even a 75-year-old table, but affordable antique chairs to put around it are plentiful.

Make Inexpensive Accessories Carry the Weight

Accessories make your house feel like a home. They define your taste and describe your experiences. Take your time in collecting these. You don't have to spend a lot of money—just put some thought into it. Souvenirs from trips, family treasures and photographs, flea-market finds—anything meaningful to you—will give your house a one-of-a-kind feel.

Pillows pack punch. Toss a few onto a couch and give it a whole new look. Making pillows is one of the easiest home sewing projects, and if you use leftover scraps of fabric, it costs next to nothing. *Hint:* For plump, comfy pillows, make the casing slightly smaller than the stuffing. Even store-bought pillows add a lot of punch for a little outlay.

Make lamps look like new. Updating a lamp is an easy way to get a new look. Buy a new shade, raise or lower the harp, change the finial, or add a wooden foot to the base. These are all inexpensive options available at any lamp shop. For a lighting-and-fixtures catalog with mail-order discounts, contact Golden Valley Lighting (274 Eastchester Drive, Room 117A, High Point, NC 27262; 800-735-3377).

Add art to your walls. Nothing adds color to a room like artwork, but paintings can be expensive. Consider instead low-priced prints, framed maps, colorful quilts, blankets, rugs, interesting plates or platters, even framed drawings by your children. Frame them yourself and save even more. Contact American Frame Corporation (1340 Tomahawk Drive, Maumee, OH 43537-3553; 800-537-0944) for a free catalog of framing supplies and do-it-yourself instructions.

☐ ☐ ☐

Addendum:

How to Throw a Yard Sale That Sells

One of the keys to running an efficient household is not to hold onto things you don't need. For something to be of value, you have to know where it is, it must have a fairly obvious use, and you should be able to reach it easily. If these conditions don't exist, it's time to purge. Most families of four can stock a yard sale every other or every third year. Here are the basics for a successful sale:

1. Don't decide today to have a yard sale tomorrow. Planning is the key to selling as much as possible. If you regularly hold yard sales, set aside a closet or space in the attic where you can store items that you want to sell. Price each article as you put it away, and when the time comes for the sale, you'll be well organized.

2. Hold the sale over at least a two-day period. If you have time, three days is best. Include a Friday, when you might get fewer but more serious shoppers, along with the weekend.

3. Be objective. Go through your whole house—including closets, attic, basement, bookshelves—and as objectively as possible list what you no longer need. Don't get sentimental. Sure, you used to love to play darts, and that antique mirror looked great in your first apartment—so cut a deal with a young person who shares your enthusiasms and watch those items be put to good use again.

4. What sells. Wooden chairs and tables, lamps, wicker baskets, patio furniture, lawn and garden tools, overcoats, appliances—preferably in their original packaging—and cutlery all sell well. Old toys and dolls might be collector's items, so if in decent shape, don't give them away. Campy is chic these days. Get out those old bowling shirts, celebrity mementos, club pins, and ties and hats. But don't try to pawn stained or broken goods—unless they're expensive or antique and can be fixed.

5. Put a reasonable price on everything. Try to assess each item objectively, but don't price things too low. If you give the impression that the goods are of no value to you, shoppers will doubt their worth, too. Besides, you want to leave room for bargaining. And you may want to lower prices on the last day to move the remaining items quickly. If you plan to sell furniture, visit antique stores to find out how much they charge for similar items. Price your pieces 25% to 50% lower; you have only a few days to sell, and you're not paying overhead costs. Visit thrift stores to get an idea of how much to charge for other items.

6. Advertise. Make up a flier that contains the pertinent information: your address (with a map, if necessary), the days and hours of the sale, the type of merchandise, and any big-ticket items that might attract customers. Photocopy it onto brightly colored paper, post the fliers in local grocery stores, on church and school bulletin boards, and on telephone poles or street signs around your neighborhood, with arrows pointing toward your house. List the same information in a classified ad in your newspaper or city magazine. The additional customers should pay for a two-day ad if you have a substantial amount of merchandise.

7. Organize smartly. Display similar items together and leave room so people can move freely. If you don't own a portable coat rack, borrow or rent one. It's easier to sell dresses, coats, and other long garments if they are hanging. Other clothes should be neatly folded on card tables. Set up a full-length mirror. Sell knickknacks at the cashier's table and set up a sign, "All items on this table: 25¢." Use hat racks, a clothesline, or hooks on the garage wall to show items you want noticed, like a quilt or piece of artwork.

8. Create a comfortable, friendly atmosphere. Talk to your customers. Have fun. Set up a refreshment table and offer cups of ice water. Or sell soft drinks, apples, and easy-to-prepare snacks like popcorn. Mothers with happy, popcorn-munching children—or husbands, for that matter—will take more time to shop.

9. Enlist some help. Even a small sale requires at least three workers: someone to man the till, someone to circulate among customers, and someone to relieve the other workers, fetch things from the house, and run errands.

10. Have plenty of change and small bills. You don't want to turn away a customer because you can't break a $20 bill.

11. Beware of people looking for more than you're selling. Keep your curtains closed and house locked during the sale. Leave no more than $50 in the till. Accept cash only.

12. Afterward, you will have leftovers. It's inevitable. Box up whatever doesn't sell and donate it to a thrift shop. Deduct the value of these goods from your taxes.

— Chapter 4 —

Appliances and Utilities

Savings in this chapter...

Accoording to the American Forestry Association, if Americans planted three well-placed trees around every home, we would save up to 50% of the national air-conditioning bill. That comes to savings of $4 billion every year. Such a measure translates into substantial personal savings as well.

As with any cost-cutting effort, reducing your utility bills requires attention to detail. Make an adjustment here, clean a filter there, replace an old appliance with an energy-efficient one, and at year's end you'll notice big savings. Take, for example, that slow drip from the bathroom faucet. You can save 50 gallons of water a month simply by replacing the worn-out washer and stopping the leak. Use a low-flow shower head (which your utility company might even give you for free) and save about $18 per person a year.

Because energy conservation is a hot topic these days, information and incentives are easy to come by. Your utility company might provide you with a free home energy audit. Con Ed, a New York power company, for example, not only sends an inspector, who estimates energy improvement costs and year-to-year savings, but also gives you a fluorescent bulb, low-flow shower head, faucet aerator, and outlet draft blocker to get you started—and it even arranges for zero- or low-interest financing to pay for improvements. Now, that's penny-pinching just waiting to happen!

In this chapter you'll find cost-cutting tips on heating (page 76), cooling (page 74), home insulation (page 70), buying and caring for appliances (page 72), and strategic landscaping (page 78). Decide what minor improvements you can make now with little or no investment; then start a priority list of the more expensive and time-consuming projects, like insulating a basement or replacing an old refrigerator. Take the tasks on one at a time, and by this summer—or next winter— your home will be in ship shape.

□ □ □

Cut Energy Costs Now

Change a few everyday habits and watch the savings mount:

Ventilating fans. Use kitchen, bathroom, and attic ventilating fans sparingly when heat or air-conditioning is active. These fans can drain a houseful of heated or cooled air in one hour.

Take showers, not baths. Believe it or not, heating water is the second-biggest energy user in your home, and baths require twice as much hot water as showers.

Don't completely dry clothes that you will iron. You'll save on the drying time, and you won't have to dampen them again.

Stop the flow. Instead of washing dishes or shaving under hot running water, fill the sink basin or a plastic tub, and turn the water off. By scrubbing in a tub, you'll use five instead of 20 gallons. By dipping your razor, you'll use roughly one gallon of water, rather than 15. Shaving in the shower requires about 27 gallons of hot water.

Buy clothes that can be washed in cold water. When clothes do call for a hot-water cycle, wash in warm instead. In most cases they'll come out just as clean.

Blow-dry. Use the air-dry cycle on your dishwasher instead of the heat-dry cycle. Do not heat-dry dishes that can drip dry overnight. Also, never run the washer until you have a full load.

Use appliances during off-peak hours whenever possible. Call your local electric company to find out the peak and off-peak hours and rate differences. One major northeastern electric company charges, during the summer, $19.67 per peak kilowatt-hour but only $3.23 per off-peak kilowatt-hour. Though the off-peak hours might be too early or late for some chores, they may not be for washing clothes or running the dishwasher.

Dry efficiently. Clean your lint filter before every dryer cycle, and your exhaust hose periodically. When these are clogged, drying time and the amount of energy used increase. Stop-and-start drying uses more energy because a lot goes into warming up the dryer. Dry loads one after another.

State Energy Office Phone Numbers

Check with your State Energy Office for energy-saving advice. Ask about scheduling a home-energy audit.

AL: 800-392-8098	KY: 502-781-7653	ND: 800-247-1493
AK: 800-478-4636	LA: 504-342-4594	OH: 800-282-0880
AZ: 800-352-5499	ME: 207-289-6000	OK: 405-521-3173
AR: 501-682-1370	MD: 410-974-3751	OR: 800-221-8035
CA: 800-772-3300	MA: 617-727-4732	PA: 800-692-7312
CO: 800-632-6662	MI: 800-292-9555	RI: 800-828-5477
CT: 203-566-2800	MN: 800-652-9747	SC: 800-851-8899
DC: 202-727-1800	MS: 800-222-8311	SD: 605-773-3603
DE: 800-282-8616	MO: 800-334-6946	TN: 800-342-1340
FL: 904-488-6764	MT: 406-444-6697	TX: 800-643-7283
GA: 404-656-5176	NE: 402-471-2867	UT: 800-662-3633
HI: 808-548-4150	NV: 702-687-4990	VT: 800-642-3281
ID: 800-334-7283	NH: 800-852-3466	VA: 800-552-3831
IL: 217-785-2800	NJ: 800-492-4242	WA: 800-926-9731
IN: 800-382-4631	NM: 505-827-5950	WV: 800-642-9012
IA: 515-281-5145	NY: 800-342-3722	WI: 608-266-8234
KS: 800-662-0027	NC: 800-662-7131	WY: 307-777-6079

For more home-energy-saving information. For free fact sheets, conservation tips, and answers to specific questions, call the Department of Energy's Conservation and Renewable Energy Inquiry and Referral Service at 800-523-2929. And write for a free copy of the U.S. Printing Office guide *Tips for Energy Savers*. Send a $1 service fee (make check payable to Superintendent of Documents) to S. James, Consumer Information Center-2C, Box 100, Pueblo, CO 81002. Ask for item No. 572Y.

The Consumer Guide to Home Energy Savings, by Alex Wilson and John Morrill, is a helpful reference. Look for it in your library, or order a copy ($8.95) from the American Council for an Energy-Efficient Economy (2140 Shattuck Avenue, Suite 202, Berkeley, CA 94704).

□ □ □

Insulating: The Basic Facts

According to the U.S. Department of Energy, air leakage, moisture infiltration, and inadequate insulation are the leading causes of energy waste in most homes built before the 1973 Arab oil embargo, and in many built since. In fact, leaks in a typical U.S. home account for 30% to 40% of heating and cooling bills. No matter how you heat or cool your house, you can save money with a relatively small investment in insulation. Caulking and weather-stripping doors and windows can save you 10% or more in annual energy costs, and it only takes a day's work and about $25 in supplies. Adding insulation to your attic and basement can save you up to another 20%.

Finding and correcting air leaks is simple. Look for joints where window frames do not meet the wall and for broken or missing putty around panes. To test a door, open it quickly: One that fits well creates a vacuum and resists the effort to open. One that opens too easily is allowing air to pass through leaks and needs sealing. Also, test windows and doors for airtightness by moving a lighted candle around the frames and sashes. If the flame dances, then you have a draft.

Check with your utility company or ask at your library for an insulation and weather-stripping how-to guide or send $3.75 for a copy of *Weatherize Your Home or Apartment* to The Massachusetts Audubon Society, South Great Road, Lincoln, MA 01773, Attention: Educational Resources.

How to Stop Air Leaks

Once you locate leaks, here's how to fix them:

Caulk. Fill spaces around door and window frames, sink and toilet pipes, and where cables enter your home.

Weather-strip. Apply thin spring metal, rolled vinyl, or adhesive-backed foam-rubber stripping (all low-cost, easy-to-install items) to windows and doors. For maximum protection against unwanted air flow (up to a 50% reduction in leakage), add storm doors and windows. Or, for a much cheaper alternative, seal out-of-the-way or non-opening windows with thick plastic, which can be bought in do-it-yourself kits for less than $5 per window and stretched with a blow-dryer for a snug, unobtrusive fit.

Use draft guards. They stop air from seeping under doors and windowsills. Make them yourself by sewing tubes out of leftover fabric and filling them with sand.

Cover air-conditioner drafts. In winter, cover the unit with heavy plastic. Secure the edges with tape.

Install a fireplace damper. If your fireplace doesn't already have one, this step alone could save you as much as $36 a year on heating bills. Or, for even better efficiency, consider glass fireplace doors.

Insulating for Dollars

It's important that you have adequate insulation, especially beneath your ground floor and in the attic. First, find out your area's recommended R-value (the resistance of an insulation material to winter heat loss or summer heat gain) by calling Owens-Corning Fiberglas Corporation's R-Value hotline: 800-GET-PINK. The higher the R-value, the more effective the insulating capability.

Then check to see whether you have sufficient insulation already in place. In the attic, where structural frame elements are exposed, look for insulation between the ceiling joists and, with a ruler, measure its thickness. To determine the R-value, consult Table 2 of the *Insulation Fact Sheet* (free from the U.S. Department of Energy, Office of Scientific and Technical Information, Box 62, Oak Ridge, TN 37830).

Also make sure your insulation is protected against moisture. The air in your house contains moisture that condenses if it passes through the insulation to cold exterior walls. The interior side of your insulation, therefore, should be covered by vapor barriers—coated paper or aluminum foil—to keep the moisture from ruining it. Most blanket-type insulation comes attached to vapor barriers, but you may have to install your own with other types of fill. Learn about the different types of insulation on the market and how to do it yourself by contacting your public utility company and by reading the *Insulation Fact Sheet.* Be sure to close your attic door and crawl-space doors and vents during winter.

□ □ □

Buying the Right Appliances

Major appliances cost a bundle to buy and sometimes even more, in the long run, to operate. You can make the ones you own more energy-efficient by keeping them clean and running smoothly. And you can save even more by buying newer, more efficient models. When you consider that a new dishwasher can last 10 years or more, a savings of $85 a year might make the investment worthwhile.

Begin by making sure all of your current appliances run as efficiently as possible. Then, as you decide to upgrade, evaluate appliances using the yellow-and-black EnergyGuide labels, which inform consumers about a unit's energy efficiency. After testing products such as furnaces, washing machines, water heaters, dishwashers, refrigerators, and air conditioners, the Department of Energy assigns either a dollar amount, which represents the estimated annual operating cost for the product, or an Energy Efficiency Rating (EER). The lower the dollar amount or the higher the rating, the more efficient the product.

New appliances are often sold on commission—with big markups—just like autos are, so after deciding on the model that best suits you, bargain. You wouldn't pay the sticker price for a new car, would you?

Buying and Installing a New Refrigerator

Consider the following tips to get the most for your money, now and through the years:

Choose the right size. Units that are too large waste energy cooling open space. Inadequate circulation causes too-small units to cool inefficiently. For one or two people, buy a model with an interior capacity of at least 12 cubic feet. For three or four people, buy one with 14 to 16 cubic feet. And for more than four people, add two cubic feet per additional person.

Pay close attention to the EnergyGuide label. Refrigerators are rated by annual operating estimates. Choose the unit in your budget range that costs the least to operate. Keep in mind that refrigerators have a long life span—an average of 17 years. When comparing the costs of various models, estimate the savings of a more efficient model over the expected life span of the unit.

Consider a two-door model. These let you open one section at a time, cutting down on the amount of cold air lost.

Give your fridge room to breathe. The condenser coils that extend behind the unit need at least an inch on the sides, an inch in back, and two inches on top (if it rests under a cabinet). Leave as much room as possible but a minimum of one foot from heat-producing appliances like stoves or dishwashers, and keep it out of direct sunlight. If it must sit near a sunny window, use a shade to block the rays.

Choosing an Energy-Efficient Air Conditioner

Air-conditioner Energy Efficiency Ratings range from 5.4 to 11.5. Anything above 9.0 is considered good. A difference of one EER point can mean more than $10 per year. To avoid wasting energy, selecting an air conditioner of the right size is also important. A unit that's too small works constantly trying to cool the space, and one that's too large doesn't stay on long enough to remove the humidity from the air. Follow these guidelines to choose the Btu (British thermal units) capacity for the room you want to cool:

1. Determine the square footage of the area to be cooled.

2. Select the nearest floor area from the Btu table below and find the basic size in Btu (per hour) for the type of outside wall you have.

3. Multiply the basic size by the following factors:

• If the longest outside wall faces north, multiply by 0.90; if it faces east, multiply by 0.95; if it faces west, multiply by 1.10; and if it faces south, there is no change.

• If the ceiling is more than 10 feet high, multiply by 1.10.

• If the room has heavily shaded windows, if it has an occupied room above it, or if the unit is to be used primarily for nighttime cooling, multiply by 0.80.

4. If the area to be cooled includes a kitchen, add 4,000 Btu. For example, if you have a 14-by-18-foot room that includes a kitchen, with a heavy outside wall, an eight-foot ceiling, good insulation, heavily shaded windows, and the longest outside wall facing east, you would need a unit with a cooling capacity of about 9,700 Btu per hour:

Basic size	East	Shaded	Kitchen	
(7,550	x 0.95	x 0.80)	+ 4,000 Btus	= 9,738 Btu

Basic Air-Conditioner Size in Btu (per hour)		
Floor area (square feet)	*Heavy outside wall**	*Light outside wall***
100	4,550	5,300
125	5,150	6,100
150	5,700	6,800
175	6,200	7,500
200	6,650	8,100
250	7,550	9,300
300	8,300	10,400
400	9,700	12,400
500 or more	11,000	14,250

*Heavy: an insulated frame wall or a masonry wall more than eight inches thick.
** Light: an uninsulated frame wall or a masonry wall eight inches thick or less.

Before buying, order the *Consumer Selection Guide for Room Air Conditioners*, with buying instructions and a comparative listing—model numbers, EER ratings, Btu, amps—of every type and brand of air conditioner you can imagine. Write the Association of Home Appliance Manufacturers, 20 North Wacker Drive, Chicago, IL 60606.

□ □ □

Stay Cool and Save Fuel

We know the hot sun can make you lazy. But in the face of exorbitant cooling costs, you must stay diligent. One way to cut your bills is simply to learn more about air conditioners—how to choose the right-size unit for your space (above) and how to keep it clean and operating smoothly. An even better way—at the risk of stating the obvious—is to learn how to avoid the heat. Use the stove more than the oven. Prepare cold dishes more often. When you do cook (or use heat-generating appliances), do it in the cooler hours of the morning and evening. Turn lights down or off during the heat of the day. (Electric lights create heat.) With a little effort, your savings will mount.

Ventilate. Be sure that attic vents are open so that the hot air and moisture that accumulate there can escape with ease. Rearrange the things stored in your attic so that a good channel exists for rising hot air. And use exhaust fans to remove heat directly from the non-air-conditioned kitchen, laundry, and attic.

Use fans to cross-ventilate, and cut down on AC use. When outside temperatures drop to comfortable levels, arrange a window fan so that it blows warm indoor air outside. The resulting draft will suck cooler air in through other open windows.

Block out sunlight. Use draperies, blinds, or shades to keep out direct sunlight. Vertical louvers, awnings, and shutters can be used outside for even greater blocking power. To find out how shade trees can save you money, see page 78.

Clean your air conditioner. At the beginning of each cooling season and each month during summer, check your air-conditioner filter. If you have a washable filter, brush it free of lint, then wash it in warm, soapy water. Allow it to dry completely before reinstalling it. With the air conditioner unplugged, examine the evaporator fins, which in most models are exposed when the filter is removed. Being careful not to bend them, vacuum the fins with a soft brush attachment. If any are bent, use a putty knife to gently straighten them. The same should be done for grills or fins on the outdoor side of the unit if this can be done safely.

Keep your bill in check. Try to set your temperature control to maintain a level no lower than 78°F. At 75°F, you are spending approximately 20% more on electricity; at 72°F, roughly 40% more. Check a thermometer that is not in the direct flow of the AC.

Start with the right AC setting. When you begin to cool a room, don't automatically set the AC on the coldest setting. Set it where you eventually want it. This cools the room just as fast and saves you money.

Battle humidity. When it's very humid outside, set the fan speed on low. This way the AC removes more moisture from the air, and you feel cooler.

Set an AC timer. If you're leaving a room with a window unit for more than two hours, turn the air conditioner off. It will take less energy to cool the room down later than it does to keep the AC running for several hours. If you want, use an air conditioner timer to turn the unit on a half hour before you return.

Keep other appliances away. Don't set electrical appliances, like a lamp or television set, too near the air-conditioner thermostat. This can cause the air conditioner to cool the room to a lower temperature than you want.

Watch the weather. Keep an outdoor thermometer in a convenient place so that you can turn the air conditioner off as soon as the temperature drops below 78°F.

□ □ □

Heat Your Home for Less

Did you know that your heated water bed uses more electricity than any other home appliance? Get rid of it! Or, if you're too attached, at least cover it with a comforter and insulate the sides. That's just one of many ways to save money on heating costs this winter. As with cooling, you'll conserve energy by learning more about the devices that heat your home, and by keeping the heat inside where it belongs. Here's how:

Lower the thermostat. For every degree you lower the thermostat during winter, you save 3% on your heating bill. Or, as one of the major petroleum companies estimates, the average homeowner can save $80 a year by lowering the thermostat from 72°F to 68°F.

Button up. Keep windows near the thermostat tightly closed so that the furnace won't be tricked into overheating the house.

Clean radiators. Dust and vacuum radiator surfaces frequently because dust and grime hinder the heat flow. When painting a radiator, use flat paint, which radiates heat better than glossy. If there are more than three layers of paint on your radiators, you should strip them down.

Use windows wisely. Keep shades and draperies open during the day to get the most heat from the sun. At night shut them to keep out the cold.

Warm clothes. The most cost-effective heating system of all is your own body, so wear warm clothes to keep the heat in. A man's body produces about 390 Btu per hour, a woman's about 330. A light long-sleeved sweater adds almost 2°F in warmth, a heavy one closer to 4°F. Two lightweight sweaters add about 5°F because the air between them acts as an extra layer of insulation.

For women, slacks. Slacks are at least 1°F warmer than a skirt. Closely woven fabrics add at least half a degree in warmth.

Don't send warm air up the chimney. To avoid losing furnace heat when you use the fireplace, close the doors to the room with the fireplace and open a window near the fireplace by up to an inch. The air needed for the fire to burn will draw from the window. The warm air from the rest of the house will stay put. If you're spending the evening around the fireplace, lower the thermostat several degrees to increase your fuel efficiency.

From a Utilities Expert: Maintaining Your Furnace

With proper maintenance of your furnace—inspecting and tuning it, checking air filters, cleaning fan blades—you can save up to 10% of your annual heating costs. If you spend $800 to $1,000 a year on heating, even a $50 tune-up leads to savings, not to mention the extended life of your equipment.

Heat pump. If you use electric-furnace heating, consider installing a heat-pump system. A heat pump uses thermal energy from outside air for both heating and cooling. Heat pumps cost anywhere from $2,000 for a house unit to $450 for a room unit. But a house unit can cut your electric bill by 30% to 40% during the cold months.

Gas heating. If you're thinking about buying a new gas heating system, ask your utility about the savings potential of electronic ignition. If you already have gas heating, ask about retrofitting your system.

Oil furnace. Have your oil furnace serviced annually, preferably during summer to take advantage of off-season rates. You'll save up to 10% on each heating bill. Also, ask the serviceman to see whether the firing rate is correct. More than likely, it isn't. Most furnaces are overfired, costing owners fuel efficiency.

Forced-air heating. Check the duct work for air leaks each year. To do this, when the fan is on, feel around duct joints for escaping air. Repair leaks with duct tape and, if necessary, with caulking. Clean or replace the filter in a forced-air heating system each month.

Landscape to Save

The National Arbor Day Foundation estimates that strategic landscaping can cut your annual home-energy expenses by as much as 25%. Plant bushy, broad-leaved trees, such as poplars, maples, and beeches, to the east and west of your house. They will shade your home during summer. And in winter, they lose their leaves, letting sun in to help heat your house.

Shade from trees is seven times more effective than window shades or curtains at reducing air-conditioning fuel costs. And shading air-conditioner compressors alone can increase cooling efficiency by as much as 10% (if you aren't using an evaporative cooler, which needs sun to operate efficiently).

In order to block winter wind, which can cause a third of a house's heat loss, plant evergreen trees close together as a windbreak on the side of your house that normally faces the prevailing winds. (If this is the same side that benefits from summer breezes, you'll need to decide which saves you more—blocking the cold or gaining the breeze.) Position the trees no more than the distance of one or two tree heights from the house.

For more information on landscaping to save money, contact your local extension office or write to the National Arbor Day Foundation, 100 Arbor Avenue, Nebraska City, NE 68410.

□ □ □

The Best Energy-Saving Devices

Heightened awareness in energy conservation has led to some useful and inexpensive energy-saving devices, like draft blockers, steam-pipe insulation, photoelectric switches, and appliance timers. The best source for such devices, Real Goods Trading (966 Mazzoni Street, Ukiah, CA 95482-3471; 800-762-7325), offers a free 55-page catalog. Here are some that will pay their way:

Shower power. Normal shower heads flow five to six gallons of water per minute. Low-flow shower heads—available at most hardware stores for less than $30—can cut that in half without appreciably changing the quality of your shower. Look for a brand that delivers no more than three gallons a minute, and (depending upon the efficiency of your water heater) you'll save five cents or more per shower. During the course of a year—given daily eight-minute showers—that's a savings of about $18 per person. Check with your utility company; it might even supply you with one for free.

Faucet aerator. Faucets often waste even more hot water than showers. Easy-to-install faucet aerators reduce the water flow by 40% to 60%, cut down on splashing, and still provide you with good water intensity. Pick up aerators at the hardware store for less than $9 apiece. Your savings will double your investment within a year.

Radiator heat reflectors. Heat reflectors, which prevent radiator heat from being absorbed by walls, cost about $6 per radiator and are generally made of a rigid plastic foam and covered by a reflective metal foil. Buy them at home centers and hardware stores and slide them between walls and radiators. You'll save between $5 and $10 a year per radiator, enough to pay for the reflectors in one season.

Lighting dimmers. Today's solid-state dimmers use little energy themselves while allowing you to conserve energy when you don't need the full strength of a lamp or chandelier. They also allow you to create a pleasant low-light ambience when you want to. A tabletop-lamp

---

BEWARE: Gadgets That Don't Save What They Claim

Energy buttons for incandescent light bulbs. These buttons, which fit into a light socket under a bulb (and leave the bulb's base dangerously exposed), chop a lamp's voltage, reducing the bulb's wattage but also reducing the bulb's output by a greater proportion. Use energy-saving bulbs or fluorescent tubes instead.

Clothes-dryer exhaust fans. Although they are supposed to vent the warm exhaust from a dryer into basements or living areas as added heat during winter, these fans often cause home moisture damage and indoor air pollution.

Quartz-tube (radiant) portable electric heaters. These heaters are costly to operate and, despite what their promoters say, do not give off more heat than other portables of the same wattage. Instead of warming room air, radiant heaters warm only what they face.

Siding insulation. These wedge-shaped foam pads fit under aluminum- or vinyl-siding panels but, because they allow air to pass behind them, offer little or no insulation. Instead, tack up large sheets of foam insulation before you install the siding.

Gas-saving devices for cars. The Environmental Protection Agency has tested hundreds and not found any that save a significant amount of fuel.

dimmer plugs into the outlet; the lamp plugs into the dimmer. Wall dimmers replace wall switches. In some states you must hire a certified electrician to install these.

Water-heater insulation blanket. If the outside of your water heater feels warm or hot, you are wasting gas or electricity. Water-heater blankets are easy to install as long as you read closely the blanket instructions and the manufacturer information for your water heater. Don't cover the power wiring of an electric water heater or the air openings of a gas-fired water heater. Your savings should cover the $15-to-$35 investment in a year.

□ □ □

Save With Smart Lighting

When you're trying to cut back on electricity use, it's easy to focus on the biggies—major appliances, home heating and cooling—but more than 16% of your electric bill goes toward lighting your home. Since most of us overlight, we can cut back without sacrificing safety. It can be as simple as dusting off shades and light bulbs (dust absorbs light) and turning off lights when you're not using them.

Saving has been made even easier by new lighting technology. For instance, the E-Lamp, hailed by experts as the first major advance in electric lighting in 60 years and scheduled to hit the market in 1993, costs about the same as a compact fluorescent bulb —$10 or $20—but last up to twice as long. And fluorescent bulbs already outlast standard incandescents by 10 times. Consider other ways to save on lighting:

Turn off the lights. A common misconception is that it takes more energy to turn a light bulb on and off than is saved by doing so. Not true. First and foremost, turn off lights when you're not using them. The constant on-and-off does not hurt the filament in incandescents, but it might weaken the ballast (the operating mechanism) in fluorescent bulbs. As a rule, if you'll be using a fluorescent light again within six minutes, don't turn it off.

Let the sun shine in. During the day, open curtains and shades to get the maximum amount of natural lighting. A 15-square-foot window receiving direct sunlight outshines 100 standard 60-watt bulbs.

Use the biggest bulb possible. One large light bulb lights a space more efficiently than several smaller ones. For instance, a 100-

watt bulb produces more light than three 40-watt bulbs and saves you 20 watts at the same time. Whenever possible light a space with one large bulb. But never exceed a fixture's designated wattage.

Use fluorescent bulbs. Fluorescent bulbs cost more, but they last up to 10 times longer and produce about four times as much light per watt as do incandescent bulbs. Kitchens, bathrooms, and workshops are all good candidates for a switch. Fluorescent fixtures are easy to install, and circular or compact fluorescent bulbs can replace incandescent bulbs in standard lamps. Use a harp extender to make room for the bulb if it is too large.

$$ Cost Comparison: Incandescent Bulbs vs. Fluorescents $$

To compare the real costs, not just the sticker prices of these two types of bulbs, you must figure for the long term.

	15-watt compact fluorescent *(bulb lasts 9,000 hours)*	60-watt incandescent *(bulb lasts 750 hours)*
Energy costs for 9,000 hours at $.08 per kilowatt-hour*:	$10.80	$43.20
Purchase price	$14.95	$7.20 (12 bulbs at $.60 each to get 9,000 hours)
Total cost	$25.75	$50.40

Total savings for fluorescent bulbs: $24.65

The national average rate.

Use energy-saving incandescents. Replace standard incandescent bulbs with energy-saving versions. You probably won't notice the difference when you replace a 40-watt bulb with a 34-watt energy saver, a 60-watt bulb with a 52-watt energy saver, and so on. Replace your 7-watt night-light bulbs with 4-watt bulbs. If you use a lamp an average of six hours a day, by reducing the wattage from 60 to 52 you save 17.52 kilowatt-hours in a year—about $1.50. Multiply that by the number of bulbs in your house (increase it for the ones that stay on all day), and you're saving an appreciable sum.

Lighten your room decor. When redecorating a room, choose lighter colors for walls, rugs, and upholstery for maximum light reflection.

Buy automatic switches for outdoor lights. Buy a photo-electric switch (about $10) that turns your outdoor lamp on at dusk and off at dawn. In the long run, your savings will cover the cost and then some.

□ □ □

How to Trim Your Phone Bill

Cutting your phone bill is as easy as making fewer calls and communicating more efficiently. It also pays to learn about what makes up your bill. Take a hard look at next month's statement and try to determine what charges can be reduced. And ask your phone company for savings suggestions. They'll be glad to help. For starters:

Use your phone book. Always check the phone book before calling directory assistance, which costs you money. In most cities, the first two to five directory-assistance calls each month are free, but subsequent inquiries usually cost 35¢ to 40¢ each. If you are ever cut off from directory assistance without getting the number, or if you are given a wrong number, call back and have the charge deleted.

Call at the cheapest time. Everyone knows that long-distance rates vary depending upon the day of the week and the time of day. But you may not know that in areas where local service charges are computed on a per-call basis, the fee for a local call also often varies according to the time of day. For example: New York Telephone discounts calls 40% from 9 P.M. to 11 P.M. Monday through Friday, and from 5 P.M. to 11 P.M. Sunday. Calls placed between 11 P.M. and 8 A.M. Sunday to Friday, from 8 A.M. to 5 P.M. Sunday, or anytime Saturday are 65% cheaper. Know the rates for your area and call during the cheapest periods.

Know your limit. Decide beforehand how much time you want to spend on a call, and stick to it as closely as possible.

Divvy up the subjects. Before the whole family makes a call to Aunt Bertha, decide who is going to ask her about her trip to Florida, who will tell her about the puppies, and so on. You can all report back on your part of the conversation after she hangs up. Not only will you save money doing this, but you'll also avoid listening to the same story several times.

Dial direct. Whether you're calling from home or a pay phone, operator-assisted calls cost more than direct calls. AT&T charges an additional $1.88 for an operator-assisted station-to-station call (a collect call, for example) and $3 for a person-to-person call. Phone cards are convenient, but a surcharge (80¢ with AT&T) is added to each phone-card call. If there's a problem with your service and you need the operator's help to make a call, be sure that you're billed at the direct-dial rate.

Compare carriers. With the fierce competition among long-distance companies these days, shopping around pays. Most now have special long-distance programs for frequently called numbers, affiliations with frequent-flier clubs, and other money-saving options. Take advantage of programs that fit in with the way you use the phone. Sprint, for example, offers a 20% discount on calls to the person you talk to the most each month. And if that person is also a Sprint user, your savings climb to 36%.

Check the bill. Carefully review your phone bill each month for mistakes or fraudulent charges. If your calling-card number has been "stolen," you'll see plenty of unfamiliar long-distance calls. Tell the phone company immediately.

Don't pay extra for an unlisted phone number. Most phone companies charge extra for you not to be listed in the phone book. Instead of paying for an unlisted number, have it listed under your middle name.

For more information. For a free copy of *How to Buy and Install Telephone Products*, a guide to different types of phones and answering machines (including a section on costs and budgeting), send a self-addressed, stamped business-size envelope to Telephone Installation, Electronic Industries Association, Box 19100, Washington, DC 20036.

□ □ □

Chapter 5

Clothing

We all know that others base their opinions of us partly on what we wear. But we seldom stop to think that the way we dress each morning affects the way we think about ourselves. Paint a picture of yourself as stylish and savvy, frugal and fun. With a little ingenuity, you can dress better for less.

Certain people look put-together no matter what they wear, while others can sport the most expensive designer fashions and look not quite right. Turning heads—or just looking smart—has less to do with your clothing budget than you might think. The secret to appearing stylish is to assess your physique, your life-style, and your wallet, and to develop a personal style that fits all three. If you really understand what you need and what you like, you can build a wardrobe that's practical and flattering without spending a fortune.

The same goes for dressing the whole family. Our special

sections for women (page 90), men (page 92), and children (page 94) can help you rethink how you shop. Did you know that the most common clothes-shopping mistake is wasting money on trendy "bargains"? Quite often when the shopping buzz wears off, you discover the deal of the century doesn't fit quite right after all. Read on to discover why white is actually the most practical color for children's apparel and why that silk dress you've been eyeing might just be a great deal.

For even bigger savings, you might want to experiment with making your own clothes. Home sewing is regaining popularity across the country. Create stylish outfits for a fraction of what you'd pay in stores, and have fun doing it. You don't have to be a pro to make your own functional and fashionable wear. See our tips for beginners on page 98 and our guidelines for buying a sewing machine on page 99.

And always remember that proper maintenance of your clothes is just as important as careful shopping. Keep your wardrobe shipshape, and add years to its life (see page 95).

□ □ □

The Basics of Buying for the Whole Family

Clothing, like food, is a necessity but also a pleasure. It's fun to buy a new outfit and to have a variety of clothes to choose from in the closet. That's why it's so easy to go over budget when shopping for clothes—especially if you're buying for an entire family. But dressing well and shopping smartly can go hand in hand. Take the time to really think about what you need, what you want, and what you can afford. Then devise a shopping plan and stick to it. Here are some pointers to help you buy wisely:

☞ **Think ahead.** Go through your closets and figure out what you need to round out your wardrobe. Get out your calendar and decide whether you'll need any new outfits for special occasions coming up in the next year. Look through fashion magazines and catalogs to get an idea of what will be in the stores and which styles you like. Make a list of the purchases you want to make, and when you're in the store, stick to it.

☞ **Buy classics.** Buying classics does not mean that you have to dress in a boring way or not be fashionable. It means recognizing your personal style, knowing what makes you look and feel good, and understanding which clothes you want to wear over and over again—for years. These are *your* classics, the clothes that you should build your wardrobe around.

☞ **Add trendy fashions carefully.** Update your look with relatively inexpensive items, such as a splashy tie or scarf to wear with your classic suit or a hip T-shirt bought in the junior department.

☞ **Always look for good workmanship.** Well-made clothes generally look better, feel better, last longer, and end up being a better value than cheap clothes. When considering a piece of clothing, check it carefully:

1. The patterns on the fabric should be correctly aligned.

2. Seams and hems should be smooth and securely sewn, and wide enough to be let out if necessary.

3. Linings should fit properly.

4. Pockets should be lined.

5. Stitches should be even and close together.

6. Buttonholes should be sewn through on both sides of the fabric, and closures and decorative trim should be firmly attached and properly placed.

7. Watch out for transparent fabrics that show the shoulder pads or seams, too few belt loops, and zippers that pucker the cloth.

☞ **The same goes for footwear.** Inexpensive shoes are no bargain if they last only one or two seasons. Your best bet is to find well-made footwear on sale. The lining of the shoe should be smooth, soft, and free of bumps and bulges. Look for smooth edges, sturdy soles, and high-quality, durable materials.

☞ **Double its duty.** Look for clothes that can serve more than one purpose. You'll get a lot more use out of a raincoat with a zip-out lining than one without. If you buy a dress that has a matching jacket, you can wear it to the office and to dinner (and save changing time, too). You and your spouse can share an oversize bomber jacket.

☞ **Heed the time frame.** If you're shopping for a winter coat, a tuxedo, or some other item you plan to wear for a long while, then you should buy the best quality you can afford in a classic style. For instance, a well-made traditional wool tuxedo should last 10 to 20 years, which makes the price—good-quality tuxes start at around $400—seem downright reasonable. If, on the other hand, you're in the market for something that's going to last only one season, like a child's bathing suit, your goal becomes reasonable quality at a low price. You should be able to spend less than $20 and get a suit that won't fall apart before summer's over.

☞ **Make sure it fits.** More clothes languish in the back of closets because they don't fit well than for any other reason. When trying on an item, study it in the mirror from all angles. Clothes can only approximate body size; we're all built differently. Make sure it fits well and that it flatters. Move around in it. Sit down. Lift your arms. Be sure it doesn't catch on any part of your body. If it's not comfortable, you won't wear it.

The only reason to buy a piece of clothing that doesn't fit properly is because you are having it altered—right away. If you can't honestly tell yourself that you'll alter it within a week, put it back on the rack. Also make sure the work is doable and within your budget.

☞ **Don't let shoes pinch.** Shoes should fit in the store. Don't buy them with the idea that they'll stretch or break in. Try on footwear in the middle of the day to allow for the swelling of your feet, and be sure to walk around, preferably on a hard surface (often conspicuously absent in shoe stores). When you're standing, your big toe should not hit the tip of the shoe. Your toes should lie flat, and the heel should fit snugly, not tightly. The shoes should not pinch anywhere. If they do or are uncomfortable in any other way, don't buy them.

☞ **Try it on the right way.** When shopping, take any items you're trying to match as well as the appropriate accoutrements. Don't wear tennis shoes to shop for formalwear, and don't try to guess whether the sweater you have on in the dressing room will look good with the pants hanging in your closet.

☞ **Buying for others.** It's helpful to keep a card in your wallet with the clothing and shoe sizes of every member of your family, but don't buy something that hasn't been tried on unless you're sure you can take it back.

☞ **Consider the upkeep.** Does it have to be dry-cleaned? That should be figured into the cost. If it requires hand washing, think about whether it's worth the extra time you'll spend caring for it. Squeeze the fabric in your hand; if it wrinkles easily, you might want to put the item back on the rack.

☞ **Return if necessary.** Be sure to keep receipts, and don't cut off the tags until you try on an item at home with other clothes. If it turns out that you don't like it or it's not as practical as you thought, take it back. Most department stores allow returns within a week or two—even on sale merchandise. Of course, if the item's color ran in the wash or it is defective in any way, return it at any time. In smaller stores, you might have to negotiate the option of returning an item. Do this before buying, and have the salesperson approve it on the receipt.

☞ **Plan ahead and shop the sales.** The best time to buy winter clothes is in January, summer clothes, July (for a complete listing of traditional sale dates, see the Penny Pincher's Shopping Calendar on page 28). Just be sure that whatever you buy is something you would want regardless of price. Getting swept up in sale mania can leave you with many useless items that add up to a tidy sum.

☞ **Be an assertive shopper.** You don't always have to take things as they come. If an item has a lipstick stain or is missing a button (and you're sure you can fix the problem), ask for a discount. Get to know the salespeople in shops you frequent and ask them to let you know about upcoming sales—or get on their mailing list if they have one. If you frequent a small store or boutique, ask the owner or manager to give you a discount or throw in a free belt on a major purchase. You never know what they'll be willing to do to retain a loyal customer.

☞ **Put designers in their place.** A designer label sometimes means better quality, but this isn't always the case. You can be sure that a designer was intimately involved in creating his or her dress collection, but other items—especially shoes, coats, handbags, jewelry, hosiery, lingerie, and bathing suits—are often created by other manufacturers who have paid to use the designer's label. Such a label is almost always accompanied by a 15% increase in price. Sometimes it's worth it, but sometimes it's not. Scrutinize a designer piece as you would any other, and don't rely simply on the famous name attached to it.

☞ **Buy in quantity.** Certain items, such as underwear and socks, are often sold at a lower price if you buy three pairs. Not only do these deals save you money, but when the dryer eats a sock, you won't have a useless single. Most department stores offer this kind of pricing, but so do some catalogs. Two good mail-order bets for underwear and socks, both based in New York City's Lower East Side, are Louis Chock (74 Orchard Street, New York, NY 10002; 800-222-0020, 212-473-1929 in New York) and D&A Merchandise Company (22 Orchard Street, New York, NY 10002; 800-338-UNDY, 212-925-4766 in New York).

Outlet Locations for Four Popular Designers

It takes a keen eye and a steady hand on the wallet to come out of a designer outlet with bargains you will actually wear. But if you're careful, you can find some incredible deals.

Anne Klein

AL: Boaz
AZ: Sedona
CA: Barstow, Gilroy
CO: Silverthorne
CT: Branford
FL: Orlando
IN: Michigan City
ME: Freeport, Kittery

MD: Kent Island, Perryville
MI: Birch Run
MO: Osage Beach
NH: North Conway
NJ: Flemington
NY: Central Valley, Lake George

NC: Blowing Rock
SC: Hilton Head
TN: Pigeon Forge
VT: Manchester Center
VA: Williamsburg
WV: Martinsburg
WI: Kenosha

Calvin Klein

AL: Foley
FL: Orlando
ME: Freeport, Kittery
MA: New Bedford

NH: North Conway
NJ: Flemington, Secaucus
NY: Central Valley, Niagara Falls

TN: Pigeon Forge
VA: Williamsburg, Woodbridge
WI: Kenosha

Liz Claiborne

AL: Boaz, Foley
CA: Gilroy
CO: Silverthorne
GA: Commerce
ME: Kittery
MD: Perryville, Queenstown

MI: Birch Run
NH: North Conway
NJ: Secaucus
NY: Central Valley
NC: Burlington
TN: Pigeon Forge
VT: Manchester

VA: Waynesboro, Williamsburg
WA: Burlington
WV: Martinsburg
WI: Kenosha

Ralph Lauren

AL: Boaz, Foley
CA: Barstow, Mammoth Lakes, Eureka
CO: Durango
IN: Michigan City
KS: Colby
KY: Eddyville
ME: Freeport, Kittery

MA: Lawrence
MI: West Branch
MO: Osage Beach
MN: Billings
NH: North Conway
NY: Cohoes, Lake George, Niagara Falls, Plattsburgh, Watertown

NC: Blowing Rock
PA: Reading
SD: Rapid City
TN: Chattanooga
VT: Manchester
VA: Williamsburg
WV: Martinsburg
WI: Appleton
WY: Jackson

Save on Clothing Staples

Shop by mail for factory rejects, which are usually only imperceptibly marred—and always less expensive. Get a free catalog of women's hosiery and underwear—some perfect, some not, most 50% off retail—from Showcase of Savings (L'eggs Brands, Inc., Box 748, Rural Hall, NC 27098; 800-522-1151).

Quinn's Shirt Shop sells irregular Arrow shirts for up to 60% below retail prices. For a price list, send $2 (credited to your first order) along with a stamped, self-addressed envelope to Route 12, Box 131, North Grosvenordale, CT 06255. Or call 508-943-7183. Both companies accept returns for any reason.

Dress for Less: A Wonderful Wardrobe for Women at Half Price

A little ingenuity can stretch your fashion efficiency. The key is to organize a wardrobe that works together. Once you succeed at that, maintain it by buying quality clothes as you find them at a discount. First, sort through your closets and pull out those things you never wear so you can learn from your fashion blunders. Then resolve to integrate those pieces you like but never wear back into active duty. Now try to expand your wardrobe with these hints:

☐ **Budget wisely.** When working out your clothing budget, try to reserve a small amount for serendipitous finds. That way, as you're searching for the "necessities" on your list, if you come across something that you can't live without, you can buy it without throwing your budget completely out of kilter. If your budget isn't realistic, you'll never stick to it.

☐ **Coordinate clothes as you buy.** Always think about what's in your closet when you're shopping. That top is no bargain if you need to buy a skirt to go with it. Instead, buy the one that you'll be able to wear with several items you already own. The idea is to make a number of outfits out of a minimum of pieces.

☐ **Keep it simple.** In general, it's better to add decoration yourself rather than buy it built-in. Beads, sequins, fur, and other decorative touches increase the cost and make an item harder to care for. Why not buy a plainer, more versatile piece of clothing and add a necklace or a scarf to dress it up in a more personal way?

Five Buys That Will Save You Money

These basics are so useful, they're a bargain even at full price:

1. A long-sleeved silk dress can be worn (in these days of overaggressive air-conditioning) year-round. Choose a style that looks good under a jacket, and you'll wear it to the office, to cocktail parties, and to weddings.

2. A black wool suit goes with just about any blouse, always looks smart, and can be mixed and matched easily. Also, black doesn't have to be cleaned as often as other colors.

3. You get an incredible amount of use out of a pair of comfortable, good-looking black leather pumps. In fact, when you find the perfect pair, you might want to buy two!

4. A wool-gabardine all-weather coat with a removable lining keeps you looking put-together and comfortable in all but the most extreme weather. Invest $300 in one that you love, and not only will it last for years, but you'll save the $475 you would have spent on a raincoat and a medium-weight winter coat.

5. A 36-inch strand of pearls—real or fake—is a true wardrobe enhancer. It can be worn in single or double strands and rivals the diamond as a girl's best friend.

☐ **Be patient.** Don't buy the latest fashions the minute they hit the magazines. Wait a month or two, and you can pick up less expensive copies of the hottest designs.

☐ **Tights are right.** In the winter, wear tights instead of pantyhose. Tights start at around $9 a pair—as opposed to $4 for hose—but most women can wear tights at least six times longer. Tights keep you warmer, too.

☐ **Creative shopping.** Women's departments are usually the most costly in the store. Shop in the men's, boys' or junior department for casual clothes and for such staples as T-shirts and socks.

☐ **Maternity-clothes alternatives.** If you're in the market for maternity clothes, be creative. Many teenagers are now wearing trapeze tops and swing dresses that leave ample room for expanding midsections; look in the junior department for stylish and inexpensive alternatives to costly maternity clothes. A long-sleeved wool tunic costs $75 or more at a maternity store, but only around $45 in a junior department.

☐ **Accessories, accessories.** Transform your outfits with clever accessories. Even something as small as a leopard-print headband can help you change your look without a big investment. Try using one or two of the following items to make last year's dress seem like new:

- a lace collar
- a colorful silk scarf around the neck
- an oversize wool shawl around the shoulders
- a knock-'em-dead hat
- an eye-catching brooch
- several strands of beads
- funky earrings
- shiny new buttons (or, for versatility, button covers)
- a striking belt
- patterned stockings or tights

☐ **Read on.** For additional ideas on getting the most for your clothing dollar, consult *Dressing Smart: The Thinking Woman's Guide to Style* by Pamela Redmond Satran (Doubleday, $19.95). It's filled with no-nonsense advice on compiling a work wardrobe, saving money, buying comfortable clothes that look good, and determining what to get rid of.

☐ ☐ ☐

For Men: Big Savings

For men, it's also best to stick with a classic look for expensive items and update with small-ticket purchases. Fortunately, the way the men's-clothing industry is set up makes that easy. Consider how long suit styles stay in fashion compared with tie styles. Take advantage of the system and the following tips, and build a quality wardrobe without a huge outlay.

☞ **Shop for discounts.** Because men's fashions stay relatively stable, it's easy for men to shop at discount stores without making costly mistakes. You can use the latest Brooks Brothers catalog as a guide, but it's also important to know your own style and to be able to recognize good materials and workmanship (see page 86). Then you can go to town at outlets, discount stores, and warehouse sales. For suits, jackets, pants, and accessories up to 30% below comparable goods, try Jos. A. Bank Clothiers (500 Hanover Pike, Hampstead, MD 20174; 800-285-2265). The catalog is free.

Shop for dress shirts by mail. Save time and money by buying dress shirts by catalog. Two good sources: Paul Fredrick Shirt Company (140 Main Street, Fleetwood, PA 19522-9989; 800-247-1417) and Huntington Clothiers (1285 Alum Creek Drive, Columbus, OH 43209-2797; 800-848-6203, 614-252-4422 in Columbus).

☞ **Buy in bulk.** When you find a good deal, stock up. Whether it's socks or suits, if you know you like it and the price is right, buy several. You might even get an additional discount on sale suits if you buy more than one.

Tux Redux

College students—or anyone else who is still growing and/or not likely to be as solicitous as he should be about the care of a tux—should consider buying a secondhand tux from a rental store. Gingiss Formal Wear shops, for instance, sell complete tuxes for three times the rental cost. That means you can get a basic black wool tuxedo jacket and trousers, plus the shirt, tie, cumberbund, studs, and cuff links, and have it tailored, for a total of $285. Even if you wear it to only one formal event per year while you're in college, you'll save $95 in rental costs. And if you were to purchase the above package at a department store, it would cost you around $575.

☞ **Use the power of ties.** For a small cost, your tie collection can make you look up-to-date on Monday, conservative on Wednesday, and casual on Friday. Holiday ties are an easy way to add zip at special occasions, and in summer a lively floral tie will garner smiles and pleasant comments at the office. A good source for ties is the chain of Tie Rack stores recently imported from England. The stores sell pure-silk ties—from conservative to splashy—at prices ranging from $11.99 to $29.99.

☞ **And accessories.** A trendy tie isn't the only way to update your look. Try funky socks, colorful suspenders, or a new pair of glasses. Hats are a relatively inexpensive way to add a lot of style to your wardrobe. They're functional, too; they keep you warm in the winter and cool in the summer, and they protect you from the sun.

☞ **Make them last.** Take care of your clothes. They are an investment. Watch what you put in your pockets (beware the uncapped pen, ruiner of untold numbers of trousers); have stained or damaged clothes cleaned or repaired promptly; and always hang your clothes immediately after taking them off. Ties should be kept on a tie rack, not jumbled together on a hook or hanger.

☞ **Shoes, too, require special attention.** If you buy top-quality shoes and take good care of them, they'll last for years, even decades, and be much more economical than a cheap pair. Quality men's shoes rarely go out of style. See page 97 for shoe-care advice.

□ □ □

Dressing Children on a Budget: It Can Be Done

A simple way to save money on children's clothes is to make sure your kids like them before you buy. Make a deal with each child that you won't buy an outfit unless both of you agree on it. Of course, that deal covers only specific items, not entire clothing categories. If your son understands he must wear a sport coat on certain occasions and he gets to help pick out one he is comfortable in, then maybe he'll wear it without a battle. And this strategy should certainly cut down on the number of pairs of pants—complete with price tag—shoved to the back of his closet. Curtail your spending on kids' clothes even more:

□ **Inventory.** Keep the same kind of clothing inventories and shopping lists for your kids that you keep for yourself. Know what you need to buy, and stick to it. Try to shop only a few times each year.

□ **Gender?** When buying for babies or toddlers, concentrate on clothes that can be worn by either sex. Primary colors are safe. Animal motifs are better than trucks or flowers. Sailor outfits look good on boys and girls and have yet to go out of style.

□ **Splash!** When buying costly items for older children, choose basic colors and accessorize with the trendy colors and splashy patterns that kids love.

□ **Buy white.** Contrary to popular thinking, white clothes are actually the most practical: They're the only ones that can be bleached.

□ **Name it.** Kids love things with their names on them, so monogram their accessories. Personalize hats, belts, bags, and the like, and keep clothing anonymous so it can be passed down.

□ **Bargain sportswear.** Athletic clothes with team names are here to stay. For a brochure of sportswear overruns at bargain prices, contact Sportswear Clearinghouse, Box 317746-V3, Cincinnati, OH 45231-7746; 513-522-3511.

☐ **Growing room.** Buy clothes that have room to expand. Look for deep hems and cuffs, adjustable straps, and elastic waistbands. If you sew, it's easy to leave extra fabric in the hem to be let down as needed. Buy shoes a half size too big for your kids. Children's feet grow every few months, and while they need well-made shoes that offer good support, they can stand a little extra toe room.

> **Knitters, take note.** If you knit, learn to make sweaters and other outfits for children from the top down so that you can add length to the body and sleeves later. For instructions, ask at your library for *Knitting From the Top Down* by Barbara G. Walker (Scribner's).

☐ **Pass it on.** Expensive and infrequently worn children's clothes, especially winter coats, snowsuits, woolens, and party outfits, are worth saving for the next child—yours or someone else's. Anything hand-knit is especially worth keeping to be passed down through the years.

☐ **Trade it in.** Children's-clothing consignment stores are cropping up all over the place. This is where you'll reap the rewards for taking such good care of your kids' clothes for all these years. While you're there, you'll probably also pick up some good-quality outfits for your kids at rock-bottom prices.

☐ **Create.** Make easy and fun repairs on children's clothing by sewing patches or bows over holes and painting designs over stains. Turn pants with torn knees into shorts. Paint dirty canvas sneakers with acrylic or fabric paint to hide dark toes. Be creative.

☐ ☐ ☐

Making Your Clothes Last Longer

Proper care extends the life of your clothes, and that means savings. Each time you undress, quickly examine your clothes for spots, holes, loose buttons, or anything else that needs repair. Then take care of it right away. It's especially important to pay prompt attention to stains, because the longer they sit, the harder they are to remove. Here are some hints to make caring for your clothes and shoes a snap:

● **Don't over-dry-clean your clothes.** The harsh chemicals used by dry cleaners can cause fabrics to fade and weaken, so dry-clean clothes only when they're soiled. And never dry-clean one part of a suit without the other; if colors do change, at least both parts will match.

● **Read care labels.** Always read the care labels on clothes, and follow the instructions if they make sense to you. If they don't, test an alternate cleaning method on a hidden area. Silks, for example, often carry a tag recommending that they be dry-cleaned, but a lot of silk clothing can (and should) be washed by hand. For example, if you own a silk blouse that you wear once a month, a year's worth of dry-cleaning it will cost you around $48 and may leave chemical residues on the silk that make it feel more like polyester. If you hand-wash that blouse in Woolite and send it to the cleaners for pressing only, you'll spend approximately $25 for a year's care—and keep your blouse in better shape. If you choose to do the ironing yourself, your annual savings per silk blouse come to a whopping $47!

● **Lower temperatures.** You don't always have to wash an item in the hottest water it will take. If it's not too soiled, use warm or cold water. It will be easier on your clothes than hot—and use less energy.

● **Use a clothesline.** In nice weather, hang your clothes to dry outside. They'll smell fresher and you'll save money.

● **Don't iron more than you have to.** Remove clothes from the dryer promptly. If they don't sit, they often don't need to be ironed. Sometimes you can get rid of wrinkles by hanging clothes in the bathroom while you take a hot shower.

● **Never iron over a stain.** The heat can set a stain and make it harder to remove.

● **Protect your clothes from spills.** Always wear an apron when cooking, and don old clothes when gardening, painting, or working around the house.

● **Store carefully.** Use dry-cleaner bags to protect out-of-season or seldom-worn clothes (except for leather and fur) from dust. Just be sure air can circulate within the bags.

● **Be prepared for rain and snow.** Don't let bad weather get the best of your clothes. When skies are cloudy, carry an umbrella and wear a raincoat and galoshes.

● **Repair if you care.** Damaged clothing, too, should be carefully assessed. Cut off a skirt with a worn hem; make a shirt with stained cuffs short-sleeved. If moths have eaten a hole in an expensive or much-cherished piece, look into having it rewoven. This highly skilled service does not come cheaply, but it is certainly worth the cost for some items.

   ● **Take extra care with leather.** Treat leather and suede shoes with weatherproofing spray, which prevents water blisters and other stains. Polish leather shoes often and clean suede shoes regularly to keep the suede from getting matted. Weatherproof all leather garments. It's also helpful to wear a scarf with leather coats or jackets to keep your body's oils from soiling the collar. Proper cleaning by a leather specialist helps leather clothes last longer; for a qualified cleaner in your area, contact the Leather Apparel Association (212-924-8895).

   ● **Dry wet shoes.** If your shoes do get wet, stuff them with paper, allow them to dry (away from a direct source of heat), and repolish them. Keep shoes well-heeled. Reheel shoes as soon as they run down. Not only does this protect the body of the shoe, but it keeps you from throwing it out of shape and breaking down the construction. Likewise, replace soles when they're worn or thin. Shoes that are worn regularly need resoling as often as every six months.

Inside Advice ✓

From a Cobbler

   1. Cushion liners or insteps can sometimes make your shoes fit more comfortably—especially if they've grown loose from wear—and they help your shoes wear more slowly.

   2. Preserve shoes by frequently applying a conditioning cream. Most cobblers recommend Meltonian, which sells for about $2.25 a jar.

3. You don't have to replace an entire heel if only a small portion is worn down; just ask for a tap. Taps generally cost a dollar or so, and your shoemaker can put them on in just a few minutes.

4. If you scuff the front of your shoes when you walk, have toe tips put on. They cost about $3 each.

5. If you damage the heel covers on a pair of shoes, take them to your shoemaker and have the covers replaced.

6. Invest in shoe trees. They maintain the shape of your shoes when you're not wearing them and can increase their life. Cedar shoe trees also absorb odors. Make sure the shoe trees don't fit your shoes too tightly, or they'll cause the leather to buckle and stretch.

7. Wear overshoes or snow boots in bad weather. Not only do rain and snow damage shoes, but salt can stain them.

Make Your Own

Sewing your own clothes has many advantages: It's less expensive than buying them already made; you can create exactly what you want; and you'll have outfits that you won't see on three other people at a party.

When you're starting out, the key is to keep it simple. Making clothes requires precision, and it's easy to get frustrated if your first project is too complicated. Besides, mistakes can be expensive when you're sewing. Rent or borrow a sewing machine for your first couple of projects. That way you can get a sense of the kind of machine you want. And if you find you don't like sewing, you haven't made a big investment. Keep in mind the following pointers as you begin, and have fun!

For starters. The first pattern you choose should have no more than eight pieces. Start with something easy and loose-fitting, like a sundress. Look for patterns marked "easy" or "very easy."

Relax. Choose a good-quality fabric that's not too expensive, so you won't be overly concerned about making mistakes.

Hide. Pick a fabric that won't show your mistakes, such as a busy floral design or paisley. Avoid stripes or plaids, which have to be matched up.

Easy does it. Use a light- to medium-weight fabric, such as cotton broadcloth, which is heavy enough to give you control but light enough to stitch easily. Don't attempt to use knits or slippery fabrics on your first few projects.

Discount Supplies by Mail

For a free catalog of buttons and sewing supplies, write or call The Button Shop (Box 1065, Oak Park, IL 60304; 708-795-1234). Taylor's Cutaways and Stuff (2802 E. Washington Street, Urbana, IL 61801-4699; 217-367-9843) has just that—scraps and handy sewing patterns. Send $1 for a brochure.

Ask for help. If you're having trouble, take a break. If the intermission doesn't help clear things up, call the salesperson at your piece-goods store. They're usually expert sewers and often can tell you what's wrong.

Take a sewing class. Courses on pattern making and proper fitting are helpful. Ask at your fabric store for recommendations. Or call the American Home Sewing & Craft Association's hotline at 800-U-SEW-NOW. Leave your name and address (with ZIP code), and the association will send you a list of teachers in your area.

Swap patterns. If your friends sew, swap patterns with them or look for or start a pattern exchange at your local library. Consider joining The American Sewing Guild, which sponsors fashion shows, seminars, and expositions on sewing. Dues are $20 for the first year, $15 after that. Contact the guild (National Headquarters, Box 8476, Medford, OR 97504; 503-772-4059) for more information.

Join a discount fabric club. For discounts of 20% to 50% on fabric, patterns, and notions, join a fabric club. Two to try: Carolynn's Fabric Center (7003-J Manchester Boulevard, Alexandria, VA 22310) and Fashion Fabrics Club (10490 Baur Boulevard, St. Louis, MO 63132).

Buying a Sewing Machine

Even if you don't make your own clothes, a sewing machine can save you money on alterations and repairs. To determine which machine is right for you, decide what you want to do—from basic hemming to fancy stitchery—then shop around. Also consider buying a used machine, especially if you might want to trade up soon. For more information, consult the following.

● The American Home Sewing and Craft Association's brochure *Guidelines: Selecting a Sewing Machine* tells how to find a dealer, features to look for, and how to test a machine. For a free copy, send a letter requesting the brochure by name and a self-addressed, stamped envelope to the association at 1375 Broadway, New York, NY 10018.

● For a chart listing sewing-machine models and their features, send $2 and a self-addressed, stamped envelope to *Sew News*, Sewing Machine Comparison Chart, Box 1790, News Plaza, Peoria, IL 61656.

● Save up to half off retail prices by shopping wholesale. Suburban Sew 'N Sweep (8814 Ogden Avenue, Brookfield, IL 60513; 800-642-4065) and Sewin' in Vermont (84 Concord Avenue, St. Johnsbury, VT 05819; 800-451-5124) both send free brochures and quote prices over the phone.

□ □ □

Chapter 6

Automobile

Savings in this chapter...

With the world moving ever faster, and people traveling longer distances more often, transportation is a major component of every household's budget. It also happens to be one of the budget areas with the potential to know no bounds. Automobile bills tend to arrive in big chunks at seemingly random times—that is, unless you take the time to regularly maintain your car and to consider all the options for buying, leasing, and renting at each juncture.

That said, your automobile and related transportation expenses provide you with the most leeway for budget tightening. Did you know that car manufacturers sell almost-new cars at substantially lower prices? (See page 103.) That a full-time student with a B average or better can get a discount on auto insurance? That the average household spends more than $1,000 a year on gasoline? That driving five to 10 miles per hour over the speed limit with underinflated tires can add $100 to your annual gas expenses? That you can use a magnet to tell whether a car has been in an accident? (See page 105.)

The average family buys a new car expecting it to last for a little more than five years. Whether it does last, what condition it stays in, and how much you get when you resell it depend largely on you. There are lemon cars, but lemon owners far outnumber them.

The auto industry and its related services—fuel, insurance, and parts—make up a huge and diverse market. There is tremendous competition, which benefits you as an educated and thrifty consumer. Every bit of frugality—whether it's a few cents on a gallon of gas, a few hundred dollars on insurance premiums, or a few thousand on the purchase or sale of a car—adds up. Preventive maintenance and smart shopping will save you money. And you don't have to be Mr. Goodwrench to do some of the work yourself.

□ □ □

Buying a New Car

With more than 600 models to choose from, you have to be well informed long before you fall into the hands of the hungry and persuasive car dealer. Armed with the proper information, however, you can make the system work for you. Remember, car salesmen have monthly quotas to fill—if you shop near the end of the month, they might be willing to give in a little easier, especially to a cagey shopper.

The Easy Four-Step Plan for Negotiating the Very Best Price

1. Once you have decided on the type of car you want, consult Consumer Reports Auto Price Service, which will tell you how much the car and accessories cost dealers. Send $11 and the make, model, and style of the car to Consumer Reports Auto Price Service, Box 8005, Novi, MI 48376. You'll receive a printout with the list price and dealer cost for the car, including the price of options.

2. Equipped with that information, visit two or three local dealers. On the lot, the list price of a car, plus all accessories— shipping, radio, automatic transmission—is pasted to the car's window. The dealer's profit is included. Compare the price to the dealer's cost on the printout, and you know what his profit margin is. More importantly, you know what his bottom line will be in bargaining.

Don't fall in love with one particular car; it hinders your bargaining ability. Start with an offer that gives the dealer a 4% profit. And don't go above 8%. Remember, the salesman is paid a commission. The more you pay for the car, the more he makes—but he also wants to make a sale. So be smart. Take your time. He'll figure out that either he makes the deal on your terms or he loses the sale.

3. Get every detail of a deal in writing—before you agree to buy—and get someone with authority, preferably a manager, to sign it. Check the Vehicle Identification Number so that if you decide to buy you can be sure you get the same car you looked at.

4. Finally, before buying, compare the quotes you get from local dealers with those provided by American Automobile Brokers, Inc., a mail-order wholesaler that is authorized to deal domestic vehicles made by General Motors, Ford/Lincoln-Mercury, and Chrysler, and foreign cars made by Alfa Romeo, BMW, Honda, Isuzu, Mercedes, Mitsubishi, Porsche, Saab, and Toyota. Price quotes include dealer prep and delivery by train or truck to a dealership near you. The first quote is free; subsequent quotes cost $3. To receive a price-quote form, send a self-addressed, stamped envelope to American Automobile Brokers, 24001 Southfield Road, Suite 110, Southfield, MI 48075; or call 313-569-5900.

References on New Cars

You should consider how the car you're looking at did in federal crash tests and weigh other important factors, like how much you can expect to pay in insurance and repairs. When making a purchase of this magnitude, buying one or more of the following references is well worth it. Or better yet, take a pen and paper to the library, find several of these titles, and take notes.

☐ *Consumer Reports'* "Annual Auto Issue," $2.95 (typically April)
☐ *Road & Track's* "The Complete '93 Car Buyer's Guide," $4.95 (November)
☐ *Autoweek's* "Autofile Annual," $3.95
☐ *The Car Book* (HarperCollins), $10.95
☐ *Edmund's New Car Prices Buyer's Guide* (Edmund Publications), published in December, February, and June, $4.95
☐ *Consumer Guide Automobile Book* (Publications International), $8.99

The Essential Car Facts for Car Buyers

Consumer Reports magazine publishes the results of its exhaustive research on new and used cars: the cheapest, the most fuel-efficient, the safest, as well as information on insurance, car repairs, the best tires, and more. For copies, contact Consumers Union Product Information at 914-378-2740.

New Car? Well, Almost

There's a new beast in the world of car buying—the "almost-new" car. Because a new car loses 15% to 20% of its value the minute it cruises off the lot, almost-new cars are often great bargains. Automakers are now selling low-mileage cars they've bought back from rental agencies, demonstration models, and cars that have been lent briefly to car-company executives or used for promotional purposes. These almost-new cars are sold through dealers and carry a steep discount along with most of the manufacturer's warranties, which can usually be extended for an additional fee to match those of new cars. Ask your dealerships about these great bargains. Driving away with such a deal can save you thousands.

Buying a Used Car

Once upon time, "used car" meant the same thing as "clunker." Today, that's changed: 16 million Americans bought used cars in 1990. For the smart and patient buyer, a used car is the best deal in town. And they're cheaper to insure.

Once you actually start scouring the "for sale" ads, the temptations are great. So first, make a prioritized list of your needs. Set the basic parameters: four doors, large trunk, V-6, manual transmission, and so on. Then consider options such as air-conditioning, power windows, and stereo. Knowing your needs, your price range, and the compromises you're willing to make—ahead of time—is the first step to finding a bargain. Set limits and stick to them.

Find out how reliable the model you're considering is by checking auto magazines for frequency-of-repair reports. Is there a local repair facility that works on it? Are parts readily available at a nearby dealer or garage? Call the National Highway Traffic Safety Administration's hotline (800-424-9393) to inquire about safety-related recalls on the vehicle.

The Basics of Used-Car Shopping

After you've done your homework, let the shopping begin. Try not to get attached to a particular car too quickly, and even if you want one badly, don't show it. Find out the car's history. Walk away from an owner who won't answer your questions. And don't rush into anything. Chances are that if you look at a car today, it'll be there tomorrow.

Look and be informed. Whether you're going to a dealer or an individual seller, show up with a pen, paper, and calculator. Let the seller know that you are informed. Have on hand relevant information about the cars you're looking at, such as the price of the car when it was new, whether it has manufacturer problems (such as recalls), and the fuel efficiency. Consult the *Retail Consumer's Guide* published by the National Automobile Dealers Association (8400 Westpark Drive, McLean, VA 22102-9985; 800-544-6232, 800-523-3110 in Virginia). This "blue book" of used car prices costs $9.95, plus $3 for shipping and handling.

Outside appraisal. Even if you are well informed, it's a good idea to have a mechanic inspect a used car before you buy it. And if you know relatively little about cars, it's essential. When you find out what's wrong with the car, use the information to bargain down the price—or to drop a lemon. If the owner won't cooperate with the appraisal, don't buy.

When buying from a dealer. Ask how long the car has been on the lot. The longer he's had it around, the more eager he'll be to sell. Dealers often have larger margins on used cars than on new ones, so don't be afraid to start low—base your offer on your estimate of the car's value, not theirs.

Some states require dealers to provide warranties for used cars with fewer than 100,000 miles on them. Most warranties cover the engine, transmission, drive axle, brakes, steering, radiator, alternator, generator, and ignition system. For details on your state's laws, write to the Attorney General's office.

What to Look For

Where was it driven? Ask the owner about the car's daily use and major trips. It's better to buy a used car with "long miles." A car with 40,000 miles accrued on highway commutes has been through

How to Inspect a Used Car

☐ **Look at the car in daylight.** The best floodlights cannot show all the defects.

☐ **Check for rust.** Run your hands along the bottom of the car body and beneath the doors. If you feel bumps or blisters in the paint or the paint is peeling, rust will soon be a problem.

☐ **Check for bodywork.** If you feel unevenness, slide a magnet along the area. Most bodywork is done with plastic, which won't attract the magnet.

☐ **Beware of stains.** Look under the car for signs of fluid leakage.

☐ **Look under the hood.** An overly dirty engine may mean it has not been well maintained. Do certain parts appear newer than others? If so, they've probably been replaced.

☐ **Start the engine.** Listen for knocks or pings.

☐ **Test-drive the car.** Drive at least 10 miles. Test the steering and brakes, both gently and with some force. Stop and check the emergency brake. Check gauges as well.

☐ **Check the transmission.** Turn the engine off, let it cool down for a minute or so, then restart it. While accelerating slowly, listen to the transmission. A hollow revving sound (in automatic-transmission cars) or a whining sound (in manuals) means the transmission is on its last legs, and a major repair lies ahead.

☐ **Test the shock absorbers.** Push down on the trunk or hood. If the car bounces more than twice, the shocks are shot.

☐ **Examine the tires.** Uneven tire-tread wear can indicate an accident or improper alignment. Uneven tread on only the front tires could indicate serious suspension damage. Check the condition of the spare and make sure all the tire-changing gear is in the car.

☐ **Investigate the odometer.** You can never be absolutely sure whether the odometer is accurate. In fact, the National Highway Traffic Safety Administration estimates that the odometer in one out of every four used cars has been tampered with, costing consumers $4 billion a year. Ask the owner to have the odometer reading certified in writing, or look for clues to corroborate the mileage shown. Check the doorjamb to see whether the mileage was recorded after a repair.

☐ **Examine the interior.** If pedals and armrests are worn and the odometer says 30,000, be skeptical.

less stop-and-go and has been turned on and off fewer times than a car that has racked up those miles over city potholes.

Who drove it? Knowing who the driver was tells you a lot. Insurance companies charge some drivers more than others for a reason. Single males under 25 pay higher premiums than males over 25 and females because they tend to do more cruising than caring for their cars. Older drivers, especially women, are usually more careful—driving slower and maintaining the car according to schedule. Don't underestimate this factor.

What repairs have been made? Proper maintenance increases a car's longevity and reduces the likelihood of major repairs in the future. An owner who has kept a maintenance journal scores big points. It's also essential to know whether the car has been in an accident. Even if the car has been repaired, an accident can cause not-easily-visible structural damage that might lead to problems down the road.

Talking Down the Price

Knowledge about the car is the best tool for effective bargaining. First, know the book value of the car, and have a feel for what the current market is like. If there are 50 others just like it in the classifieds, it's a buyer's market, and you stand a better chance of successful haggling. Now start deducting for the negatives of this particular car:

☐ **Dead shocks.** If one set of shocks is bad, deduct between $60 and $125; double it if you'll have to replace both sets. For small American cars, figure closer to $60; for larger American and foreign cars, $100; for top-quality shocks, $125.

☐ **Worn-out tires.** If the car needs new tires, take off another $200 to $400, depending on the size and quality.

☐ **Missing parts.** A broken mirror or a missing hubcap might not seem like much at first glance, but it all adds up. Lower the price by $75 for the mirror, $25 for each hubcap.

☐ **Worse for the wear.** You can't really put a price on problems such as rust, worn seats, and general wear and tear, but if you tick them off before making a low offer, you'll be taken more seriously.

From an Auto Mechanic: Never Buy a Used Car That...

Inside Advice ✓

Used-car buyers run the risk of inheriting someone else's mechanical problems. Never buy a used car...

☞ **that is rusting in the interior or on the underside.**
Exterior rust is a sign of what's to come. Interior rust is a sign of what is. Check in between doors and seams, and underneath the trunk. If rust eats through the trunk, exhaust fumes can travel into the passenger compartment.

☞ **that leaks fluid.** A car should not leave behind puddles of water, oil, or transmission fluid.

☞ **with brakes that don't operate smoothly.**

☞ **with a noisy engine.** Listen for rattles, sputters, and squeaks.

☞ **that smokes.** Small puffs of white vapor are okay, but when test-driving, keep your eyes peeled for other, more drastic smoke signals.
Blue smoke = burning oil, costly repairs.
White smoke = possible crack in engine block or cylinder head.
Black smoke = adjustment in fuel system needed.
Billowing white smoke = possible crack in engine block or cylinder head, or blown gasket head.

☞ **that has a musty odor in the interior,** which means there's a leak in the roof. Repairs are costly.

☞ **that has been seriously wrecked.**

☞ **on a verbal agreement.** Get everything written in ink.

Selling Your Car

Use the information in "Buying a Used Car" (page 103) to help you determine the price to ask for yours when the time comes. By all means, keep a maintenance journal for evidence of good care, and keep receipts for all major work. If you have replaced half the car over the years, you want to get some credit for that when you sell it.

How to advertise? Placing a classified ad in your local newspaper is the easiest way to sell a car. But if you have to run the ad for weeks, it gets expensive. Try parking your car in a high-visibility location with a "for sale" sign and your phone number well displayed. If this location is your home or office, all the better. Also, post signs on bulletin boards at drugstores, grocery stores, health clubs, and in other high-traffic areas.

Pricing to sell. If you haven't put an extraordinary amount of miles on your car and have kept it in good order, ask 15% to 20% above the "blue book" value. Ask slightly more than you expect to get, but not so much that you scare people off. If there are obvious problems with the car, type out on a sheet of paper the base price of the car, minus deductions for the problems, to show how you came up with your very reasonable asking price. Your negotiating position has just become much more solid.

Be prepared. Have the facts at your fingertips when people call: model, year, mileage, fuel efficiency, and recent improvements. And stress the positive aspects of the car: excellent condition, AM/FM stereo, garaged, air-conditioning, one driver, low mileage, or whatever attributes apply. Keep the car clean inside and out at all times. The prospective buyer's first impression has a great impact.

Be confident. Encourage the buyer to look at your car during daylight. Encourage him or her to drive it. Open the hood. Stress the fact that the car is well maintained.

Negotiate, yes. But don't cave in. Use the fact that you kept the car in good order to keep the price up. Don't go below your predetermined bottom line, but be reasonable. Don't let negotiations snag over a few bucks just on principle. Consider the value of your time.

□ □ □

Preventive Car Care

Car repair can be expensive, time-consuming, and inconvenient. The best way to avoid the hassles and costs of major work is to fix the little problems as they occur. Your owner's manual is the place to start. Read carefully the suggested maintenance schedule and stick to it. Shelling out a little bit for preventive care will save you many times the amount in the future. Besides, it's more convenient for *you* to determine when your car will be in the shop than for *it* to do so. When you decide to sell, you'll reap even more financial benefits from your careful maintenance.

Easy maintenance checklists. Like most chores, maintaining your car becomes second nature once you get used to it. So take the time to have a mechanic or knowledgeable friend explain where everything is. Ask questions until you really know what's going on. Run through the following checks once a month, or more often for older cars:

- Check engine oil.
- Check transmission fluid.
- Check power-steering fluid.
- Check drive belts for excessive wear and to be sure they are not too tight or too loose.

Once a month, when the engine and tires are cool:

- Check coolant level in radiator.
- Check fluid level in master brake cylinder.
- Check air pressure in tires and look for wear and tear or irregular friction.
- Check (in a garage or at night) headlights, taillights, directional signals, and brake lights.

Tune-ups. You should tune up your car every 10,000 to 12,000 miles. Tuning up and regularly replacing parts can be done yourself with the aid of a manual, or use a trained mechanic whom you know and trust. You'll spend $100 or less, and you'll save thousands.

Do-it-yourself repairs. Helm Inc. (800-782-4356) distributes owner's manuals and repair books for the major automakers. Call and tell them the manufacturer and model number of your car, and they will send you the appropriate manual. Prices vary. Helm serves most domestic cars, along with Honda, Isuzu, Mazda, and Acura.

Join an Auto Club

If you drive long distances frequently, or if you own an older car or have several young drivers in your family, you might want to join an auto club. The national clubs listed below have competitive prices—ranging from $40 (individual) to $85 (family policy) per year—and offer similar services, including emergency road service, route planning, and hotel discounts. Call to find the deal that best suits your needs and location. Study a club's brochures before you join.

AAA. Look up AAA locally or call 800-AAA-HELP.

Allstate Motor Club. 800-323-6282.

Amoco Motor Club. Half-price hotel-motel plan at 1,500 establishments. 800-334-3300.

Cross Country Motor Club. 800-225-1575.

U.S. Auto Club. 800-348-5058.

Montgomery Ward Motor Club. 800-621-5151.

Free helpful hints. Shell Oil Company publishes a helpful series of booklets about car care, with special tips on operating an environmentally friendly car, being a smart driver, helping injured drivers, and more. For a free copy, write to Shell Answer Books, Shell Oil Company, Box 4681, Houston, TX 77210.

How to Buy Tires Wholesale

Save up to 35% by ordering tires from Belle Tire Distributors, Inc., which has been in business since 1922. Belle sells only new tires made by Bridgestone, Firestone, B.F. Goodrich, Goodyear, Kelly Springfield, Michelin, Pirelli, Uniroyal, and Yokohama. Call or write for prices (Belle Tire Distributors, Inc., Wholesale Division, 3500 Enterprise Drive, Allen Park, MI 48101; 313-271-9400.)

Choosing a mechanic. Ask friends and neighbors for the name of a dependable mechanic. Check to see whether any complaints have been filed against him at the Better Business Bureau. For the first few jobs, get second opinions, especially for major work. As you get to know and develop trust in your mechanic, he'll be more likely to charge reasonable prices. Be a friendly face and show knowledge and concern for your car.

Maintenance diary. Keep a diary in your glove compartment. Include the checklist from page 108 and the dates and specifics of executing the items on the list. Record the dates you change fluids, tires, wiper blades, etc., and prices for service. Keep a brief record of regular highway commutes and long highway drives. Your diary tells you how things are changing, when you're due for a tune-up or oil change, which brand of oil or what size fan belt you last bought. You'll be rewarded when it comes time to sell the car or when you're trying to persuade the insurance agent that you're a good car owner who deserves a lower premium.

Keeping your car clean. You don't need to buy a lot of fancy formulas with hefty price tags. For a real gleam, wipe chrome and stainless steel with a soft cloth moistened with white vinegar.

Dirty windshield? Baking soda sprinkled on a wet sponge does a terrific job cleaning road grease, grime, and bugs from windshields and headlights. If elbow grease and baking soda don't seem up to the task, attack first with onion bags, the net kind, which are abrasive enough to scrape away any caked-on matter but won't damage your windshield. Follow with the baking soda and a good rinse. (Baking soda in the bottom of your ashtrays prevents discarded cigarettes from continuing to burn.)

Be Prepared

In a magnetic case under the bumper, hide a spare set of ignition and door keys. In your trunk, store a little emergency kit. More often than not, the problem on the side of the road is something you can handle yourself—a flat tire, a broken belt. Tow trucks and repairmen charge a pretty penny for road calls and can be hard to contact. You should carry and know how to use the following equipment: ☞ First-aid kit ☞ Flashlight ☞ Spare tire ☞ Jack ☞ Four-way lug wrench ☞ Spare belts ☞ Tire-pressure gauge ☞ Wrench and socket set ☞ Screwdriver ☞ Pliers ☞ Utility knife ☞ Jumper cables ☞ Fuses ☞ Hose clamps ☞ Water ☞ Motor oil ☞ Aerosol can of air to inflate tire ☞ Fire extinguisher ☞ Rags

---

How to Go Farther on a Gallon of Gas

By minimizing resistance and drag, increasing engine efficiency, and using careful driving techniques, Shell Oil Company Mileage Marathon drivers drove a car nearly 400 miles on a single gallon of gas. Impossible in your car, yes, but there's certainly a lesson to be learned.

Today's autos are far more energy-efficient than the ones we drove as recently as the 1970s. Steps for decreasing gas use have changed as well. In the 1970s, for example, drivers were encouraged to replace belted tires with radials to increase fuel economy. Today, almost all cars come equipped with radials. You simply need to keep tires properly inflated.

Buying the right car. The Environmental Protection Agency and Department of Energy's fuel-economy label gives the estimated miles per gallon (mpg) of vehicles. The free EPA/DOE *Gas Mileage Guide* can be obtained at most car dealerships or by writing to Consumer Information, Pueblo, CO 81009. The Better Mileage Company (Box 40063, Tucson, AZ 85717) offers advice on fuel efficiency and sells related products. Write for a free brochure.

Buying a car that gets one mile per gallon more than another can save $400 over the life of the car. Based on the EPA's *1992 Gas Mileage Guide*, the average fuel economy for autos is 28.1 mpg. The GEO

Metro XFI is the most fuel-efficient car, rated at 58 mpg highway, 53 mpg city. The least is the Lamborghini, rated at 14 mpg highway, nine city.

Do it yourself. Save up to 20¢ a gallon by pumping your own gasoline at the station. When doing so, stop when the pump automatically shuts off. Spillage wastes fuel that *you* are paying for. It also eats through car paint.

Leave your car at home. It's always a good idea to walk or ride a bike whenever it's convenient. In addition to giving you good exercise, it's the ultimate gas saver. Carpool or use mass transportation whenever possible.

Fill 'er up—with low test. Most cars do not need high-octane fuel to run efficiently. Some 80% of all vehicles operate effectively on 87-octane gas, without loss of economy or durability and without increased emissions. In fact, low-octane fuel is good for energy conservation, because it requires less crude oil per gallon than do premium fuels.

Use the right oil. Use the lowest-viscosity oil recommended for your car by the manufacturer. If it's designated "EC II," then it's an energy-conserving oil.

Warm it up. A cold engine uses nearly 20% more gas than a warm one, so warm up your car briefly, drive slowly at first, and do as many chores as possible at centrally located stops.

Don't be an idler. An idling engine consumes up to a half gallon of gas per hour. In most cases, you're better off turning off the car. In general, it takes less gas to turn it back on again than it does to leave the engine running for more than a minute.

Travel light. If you're tempted to use your trunk for storage space, remember that it costs you money. Leave your golf clubs and extra tools at home when you're not using them. But when you're traveling, fill up the trunk and spare passenger areas before adding luggage racks or trailers. These add drag, considerably reducing fuel efficiency and increasing wear and tear on your car.

Be sparky. Worn-out spark plugs cost you up to 25% of your fuel economy. For better start-ups and smoother idling, keep your engine tuned up. The average annual savings per household is a mile per gallon, or $53. Save another mile per gallon by replacing a clogged air filter.

Fresh air. Roll down the window to cool down. Use the air-conditioning as sparingly as possible. But never do both.

Drive within the speed limit. The average household saves up to $25 a year by driving within the speed limit. For every mile per hour above 55 mph, the average vehicle loses more than 2% to 3% in fuel economy. A car that gets 28 mpg at 55 mph will get 21 mpg at 65 mph. Smooth acceleration can save you up to another two miles per gallon in the city. Oh, and speeding tickets don't help either.

Keep tires inflated. Underinflated tires waste gas, as do unaligned ones. The Energy Department estimates that properly inflated tires can save the average car owner 2% to 3% of each gas bill. Keep a tire-pressure gauge (available at automotive stores) in your glove compartment, and check your tire pressure once a month. It's easy to do, and it prolongs the life of your tires and engine. Check the tire itself or the sticker on the driver's-side doorjamb for the recommended air-pressure level—probably between 26 and 36 pounds per square inch (psi). When the tires are cold, take a pressure reading. *Note:* Don't rely on borrowed gauges, particularly those at gas stations, which are often inaccurate.

> **Bargain:**
>
> To order the **Tire Safety and Mileage Kit**, which includes a pressure gauge, a tread-depth gauge, four tire-valve caps, and a consumer tire guide, mail a check for $4 to Tire Industry Safety Council, Box 1801, Washington, DC 20013. Or you can send a self-addressed, stamped envelope for the free guide only.

□ □ □

Insurance Savings

After buying a car, choosing insurance is the most expensive and complicated aspect of owning one. Among—even within—insurance companies, you can be quoted huge differences in premium prices. Shopping around is a must. According to a chart published in the *Virginia Auto Insurance Consumer's Guide*, which shows the premium rates and payouts of 50 of Virginia's largest insurance companies, an unmarried 20-year-old female will pay $4,763 annually (1991 figures) for coverage with Integon General but only $717 with Erie

Insurance Exchange.

While some factors are beyond your control, it's important that you know what to ask for and how to get the discounts you're entitled to. Where you live and work and how you drive matter. Often, whether you smoke matters: Smokers pay more. If you drive less than 7,000 miles per year, participate in a car pool, or have your car equipped with automatic seat belts, air bags, or antilock brakes, you'll reduce your rate.

Get price quotes from at least five different insurance companies. They'll require all the necessary facts—age, area, drivers, driving records. Let them know the factors that can get you discounts. Assess your record carefully with your insurance agent, including how many miles you drive. Be sure he knows it if young drivers to be included on the policy have taken driver-education courses or if they have B averages or better in school.

Learn before you shop. *Consumer Reports* publishes the results of its research on auto insurance, with details on the cheapest rates, the fastest-paying companies, and more. For a copy, write to Consumers Union Reprints, 101 Truman Avenue, Yonkers, NY 10703-1057.

Other factors to consider. If you're insuring more than one car, try to get a cheaper rate. Find out whether you get reduced rates if you carry homeowner's insurance, life insurance, or another type of policy with the same company.

Over time. Stay with the same company and keep a good record (no accidents, speeding tickets, or other moving violations), and eventually you can save up to another 25%. But do comparison-shop every couple of years to make sure your policy has stayed competitive.

Cancel unneeded policies. When you sell your car, save hundreds of dollars by canceling the insurance the day the title passes. Many people forget to do this and end up paying extra.

More Cost-Cutting Auto Insurance Tips:

☐ When renewing your policy, **consider raising the deductible** on the collision and comprehensive (theft, vandalism) portions of your coverage, or even dropping them if the old family wagon is well past its prime.

☐ Compare your auto policy's medical coverage against your health insurance for overlap. If state law allows, and you're certain your health policy is sufficient, you can **drop the duplicate coverage.** Be sure to hang on to your liability coverage, though.

☐ Families in the market for a new car should keep in mind that air bags, automatic safety belts, antilock brakes, and other **safety features mean lower premiums.**

☐ **Take advantage of low-mileage provisions** (for people who don't regularly drive long distances) and safe-driver clauses (for family members with no moving violations), as well as car-pool and two-car discounts.

☐ **For more information,** call the National Insurance Consumer Helpline (800-942-4242).

☐ ☐ ☐

The Ins and Outs of Renting a Car

So many kinds of discounts exist for renting cars that you should almost never pay full price. If you have a bank account or if you're a member of a frequent-flier program, museum, club, retirement group, corporation, or professional organization, you probably qualify for a car-rental discount. Check with your associates and with the rental agencies to see whether any of your memberships qualify you for these discounts. As far as the rate goes, in major urban areas, check to see whether there are different rates, say, if you pick up the car at the airport rather in midtown.

Most states have laws that guarantee you a car if you have reserved one. When you make a reservation (always get the reservation number) and show up within a half hour of the time, the company is required to give you a car of similar size or a free upgrade if the one you reserved is not there. Or they must pay for transportation to another office or agency (it varies state by state). If it is to another rental agency, the original agency must pay any increase in cost.

Basics of Frugal Car Renting

1. Use toll-free phone numbers to **comparison-shop**. Look for weekly and weekend specials.

2. Ask whether there are extra **pickup and drop-off fees** at the locations you will be using.

3. Find out about any **blackout dates** that could affect an advertised special.

4. Ask about the **weekly rate** if you're considering a rental for more than four days. The daily rate for rentals of more than four days, but fewer than seven, is often higher than renting a car at the weekly rate.

5. Ask about **mandatory additions** to the quoted prices, such as mileage rates and caps, fuel charges, airport surcharges, and taxes. Also, ask about other optional charges when they're applicable, such as additional-driver fees, underage driver fees, out-of-state charges, and equipment-rental fees. Always check about the gas policy. Sometimes a tank of gas is included, but more often you have to return the car full. Agencies charge a substantial markup when it's your responsibility and you forget.

6. Ask about charges for optional **collision damage waiver** (CDW), personal-accident insurance (PAI), and personal-effects coverage (PEC, also known as personal-effects protection, or PEP). Know whether your own auto-insurance policy or credit cards cover these.

The Great Rental-Car Insurance Question

For many years, rental-car companies made a tidy profit selling insurance policies to renters, but recently credit and charge cards have provided such insurance at no cost when you charge the rental. Paying with a credit or charge card usually provides the renter with insurance for damage, theft, and liability. But beware! Up to 25% of rental-car claims made against credit cards are rejected because of violations to the contract: a second driver was not listed on the rental agreement; the driver's license had expired; or the driver was speeding.

Your best bet is your homeowner's policy. Some—for instance, Chubb in New York—cover rental cars. If you own and insure a car, call your agent to find out whether your policy covers rental cars. The deductible is usually much less for rental cars, so don't let them tell you otherwise if it is written in your contract.

What You Get From Your Credit or Charge Card

Below are some services the cards provide if you use them to pay for the rental. These benefits are subject to change, so before relying on insurance from a credit or charge card, check with the financial institution first.

American Express. American Express suggests you decline collision insurance from the rental company when paying with the American Express Card. American Express provides collision coverage up to $40,000 on the green card and $50,000 for the gold card. It does not cover liability, and the coverage is secondary to any other insurance that may apply, such as homeowner's or car insurance. Coverage ends after 15 days (31 overseas), so if you're renting for an extended period, either purchase the necessary additional insurance, or, if there is no rate penalty, turn the car in at 15 days and rent another.

Diners Club. Diners Club offers up to $25,000 for collision, and coverage is good for the duration of the rental period. The advantage of the Diners Club coverage is that it is primary. Even if another policy that you have would cover the damages, Diners Club insurance will still pay for them.

Visa. Most gold Visas and MasterCards offer secondary coverage. Visa/MasterCard collision insurance covers up to the value of the car. Coverage is for 30 days. Some non-gold Visa/MasterCards provide coverage, but others do not. Ask the issuer of your card for written information.

☐ ☐ ☐

— *Chapter 7* —

Staying Healthy

Savings in this chapter...

Whether you're shopping for prescription drugs, over-the-counter products, beauty aids, or a new health plan, there are plenty of ways to save when it comes to matters of health. For instance, did you know that your HMO probably offers you a substantial rebate for joining a health club? You probably didn't. Most don't go out of their way to tell you. U.S. Healthcare refunds $200 per person on its plan. We show you other ways to economize on your health-insurance costs on page 131.

Of course, it's better simply to stay healthy. You know what they say about an ounce of prevention. And you don't have to spend a lot of money on diets and health gizmos to do that. Don't even think about taking fish-oil supplements (Americans bought $35 million worth last year). But if you're over 50, you might want to take an aspirin every other day to reduce your risk of having a heart attack (ask your doctor first). And do exercise, no matter what your age. The simpler you keep your exercise routine, the more effective it will be, primarily because you have a better chance of sticking to it.

For those times when you do succumb to some marauding illness, your first instinct is often to head to the pharmacy to purchase relief. (That's why the stock prices of pharmaceutical companies never seem to be affected by recessions.) But that's one illness the successful penny pincher must learn to overcome. To help you, we have listed the 10 best home remedies (page 122): cures you should try—except in emergencies—before seeing the doctor. These really work. No witches' brews, and you don't have to have a Ph.D. in botany either.

When it comes to shopping for drugs and beauty aids, if you're buying name brands at drugstores, you're paying at least 36% too much and probably far more. (See our national brand vs. store brand price-comparison chart on page 126.) And that's just for starters. Many expensive products, like eye shadow and moisturizer, come from common substances you can buy yourself with no inconvenience— because they are sold right there at the very same drugstore. In such cases, you are paying 200% to 500% above cost for name brands. Believe us, you don't have to be a scientist to save big.

□ □ □

An Ounce of Prevention...

The best way to save on health-care costs is to keep yourself in good shape so that you don't get sick in the first place. Taking steps toward better health doesn't have to be confusing or complicated. The most important components of a healthy life-style are simple: Maintain a positive outlook and keep a sense of humor, exercise regularly (bonus: you'll sleep better), and eat sensibly. For staying in top shape without spending a lot of money, here are some basic tips and some traps to avoid:

□ **Secretly frosted flakes.** The best days really do start with breakfast. Cereal with skim milk is your best choice, but shop carefully. Dozens of breakfast cereals claim to be "whole grain" or "all natural," but these terms can mislead. Many are loaded with sugar, salt, and even fat. Raisin bran can contain as much sugar as some sugar-coated cereals, and granola usually contains at least 25% fat.

There is good news, however. Two cereals that are low in sodium and that contain nothing but the grain also happen to be the least expensive: puffed wheat and puffed rice. Many supermarkets carry their own brand of puffed cereals, inexpensively packaged in plastic bags, which cost about a third of what most name-brand cereals cost. And a cup of puffed rice weighs in at a mere 50 calories, so you can feel free to top it with a sliced banana or handful of berries.

☐ **Make meat a supporting actor.** Meat has gotten a bad rap lately as an enemy to good health. But you can still enjoy it while maintaining a healthy diet. The trick in serving meat is to shift the balance—from main dish to side dish. Vegetables and grains, which are both better for you and cheaper, should be the main attractions. For example, serve steamed broccoli over brown rice as the main dish, accompanied by three ounces of lean beef or pork. Or add a similar amount per person of either sliced boneless chicken or shrimp to a vegetable stir fry.

☐ **Wonder veggies.** Vegetables win hands down as the best way to fill up on few calories and few dollars. Fresh vegetables outrank frozen and canned in vitamins and other valuable nutrients that can be lost during processing. Cruciferous vegetables are now widely believed to help prevent certain kinds of cancer. Look for dark-green and yellow vegetables, including these nutritional powerhouses: broccoli, cabbage, cauliflower, Brussels sprouts, carrots, and kale. To cut costs, buy what's in season and shop at farm stands when convenient. For more information, call the American Institute for Cancer Research Nutrition Hotline, 800-843-8114. Ask for a free copy of "Menus and Recipes to Lower Cancer Risk."

Dietary Guidelines for Lowering Cancer Risk

1. Reduce the intake of fat, especially saturated fat, to a level of no more than 30% of total calories.
2. Eat plenty of fruits, vegetables, and whole grains.
3. Eat salt-cured, pickled, and smoked foods in moderation.
4. Drink alcoholic beverages in moderation, if at all.

☐ **A pepper a day.** Studies show that vitamin C can ward off illness and nip a cold in the bud. A supplement can provide 10 times the Recommended Daily Allowance, and citrus fruits and cantaloupe are good sources. The green pepper is loaded with this valuable vitamin and makes a low-cost crunchy snack with too few calories to bother counting. Don't fall for the vitamin C "candies" sold in checkout lines; their C content is low, and they're full of sugar. *Note:* When you do need vitamin supplements, call The Vitamin Trader (800-334-9310), which offers discount prices.

☐ **The cheapest form of therapy.** Necessity is not just the mother of invention, it is a sustainer of life. Give grandmothers and grandfathers children to baby-sit on a regular basis or a pet to care for, and they will live longer. Older people with pets have been proven to get sick less and heal faster. The company of a dog not only helps lift spirits and calm nerves, but it provides a built-in exercise program of walks and play. Dogs are best, but any living creature to care for can brighten someone's day. *Note:* See page 157 for information on adopting a pet at your local SPCA.

☐ **Exercise.** Regular exercise helps prevent problems in at least five important areas: coronary artery disease, obesity, osteoporosis, depression, and non-insulin-dependent diabetes mellitus. The trick to maintaining a regular workout program is to turn exercise into something that is fun and easy to fit into your daily schedule. You'll feel stronger, more flexible, and more energetic. For free information about the ideal workout for you, call the President's Council on Physical Fitness and Sports (202-272-3430).

Five Tips for Establishing and Maintaining a Workout Program

1. Pick a method of exercising that you enjoy.
2. Set reachable goals and work at a steady pace to achieve them.
3. Keep a chart of your progress.
4. Vary your routine.
5. Exercise with friends on a regular schedule.

Save on Exercise Equipment

Order free catalogs from these discount houses for low prices:

✔ For bicycles and stationary bikes, call Bike Nashbar, 800-NASHBAR.

✔ For rowers, treadmills, stair climbers, and other equipment, call Creative Health Products, Inc., 800-742-4478.

✔ For croquet sets, golf clubs, and balls for all sports, try Bennett Brothers, Inc. (the $5 charge for the catalog is redeemable), 312-263-4800.

☐ **Hoofing it.** People are rediscovering the oldest workout known to man: walking. Walking is easy on the joints and back and is ideal for folks of all physical abilities. It's a great stress reducer, providing a peaceful time to think or chat with a friend, and it requires little if any special equipment. Start with a half-mile trek and gradually build up distance and speed. For the best workout, move your arms as well as your legs, and carry hand weights if you like. A mile of walking burns up about the same amount of calories as a mile of running.

☐ **Preventing disease.** Doctors are currently recommending several preventive measures that are as enjoyable and inexpensive as eating wisely. In fact, that's exactly what they involve. Just remember: All things in moderation.

● **Cancer.** Researchers in Israel have determined that the spice cumin, widely used in Indian and Mexican dishes, is the most active of several spices thought to help prevent cancer. Tests show that cumin increases the activity of GST, a cancer-blocking enzyme produced by the body. *Tip:* Save more than 50% on spices by buying them in bulk at health-food or spice stores. You can still buy small amounts, you just forgo the nice bottle. Save old spice bottles and refill them cheaply. Also, buy spices in relatively small quantities, since many of them, including cumin, decrease in potency with age.

● **Heart disease.** Researchers have speculated for years that moderate alcohol consumption may improve circulation and decrease the risk of heart disease. Red wine in particular may contain a potent anticarcinogen called quercetin. We're not encouraging anyone to start drinking, but if you enjoy a glass of wine every now and then, there's no reason to stop. It makes sense to indulge at home, though, since the restaurant markup on wine can be anywhere from 50% to 100%.

● **Viral infection.** The healthy bacterium that turns milk into yogurt may have yet another notch in its belt. Studies show that people who eat yogurt have an increase in gamma-interferon, a compound produced by the white blood cells that fights viral infections and may also block cancer. At any rate, yogurt is an inexpensive source of calcium and low-fat, high-quality protein.

☐ ☐ ☐

Mother Nature's Medicine Chest
Our 10 Best Do-It-Yourself Remedies

When minor ailments get the better of you, try these homegrown tips before heading out for expensive store-bought medications. But be sure you know the signs of serious illness: persistent headache, chronic cough, fever for more than three days, sore throat for more than two days, any pain that lasts longer than seven days, or headache or sore throat accompanied by fever, rash, nausea, or vomiting. Don't hesitate to call your doctor when necessary.

You can easily grow many of the herbs we mention in your backyard. Or try these bargain suppliers: Great Lakes Herb Company (Box 6713, Minneapolis, MN 55406) for organic herbs and seeds; Herbalist and Alchemist (Box 553, Broadway, NJ 08808) for teas, books, and herbs; Hartenthaler (133 Henderson, Norwood, PA 19074) for herbs, spices, teas, extracts, essential oils, and books.

☞ **Athlete's foot.** Cure athlete's foot by soaking feet once a day in a solution of half a cup of apple-cider vinegar and two cups of hot water, until the water cools. It takes about a week to work, but the acidity of this solution is effective in killing all but the most stubborn of fungi.

☞ **Cold, headache, and minor fever.** Try a cup of rosemary tea to relieve headaches and cold symptoms. Brew two tablespoons of dried rosemary leaves (either in a tea ball or loose) in a cup of boiling water for at least five minutes, then strain. Dogwood-bark tea is another popular remedy for colds and fever, especially when combined with a couple of days in bed and lots of fluids. The bark can be scraped from the tree with a pocketknife, but be sure the tree has not been sprayed recently with pesticides. And take care not to dig all the way down to the pulp, damaging the tree. To make the tea, rinse the bark, then put a teaspoon or two in a tea ball. Place it in a large mug and pour in boiling water. Steep until the water becomes slightly yellowish. Add a little lemon or honey, and enjoy!

☞ **Cough, sore throat.** The ancients credited horehound with the power to cure everything from snakebites to typhoid. Although it's best known today as an old-time candy flavoring, horehound has merits as a cough and sore-throat remedy. These days, horehound lozenges are as hard to come by as a general store, but you can make an inexpensive and palatable cough syrup by mixing strong horehound tea with honey. Steep a quarter cup of dried horehound leaves in one cup of water until it cools. Stir the tea into two cups of honey, and bottle tightly. Take a spoonful at a time, up to six times a day.

☞ **Indigestion.** For a delicious alternative to "plop, plop, fizz, fizz," add a heaping tablespoon of freshly grated cinnamon and a spoonful of honey to a cup of boiling water. Parsley can also settle the stomach and is widely known as an effective diuretic. *Bonus:* Parsley is a natural breath freshener.

☞ **Motion sickness.** Try ginger root, which can alleviate nausea without drowsiness. Steep two tablespoons of grated ginger in one cup of boiling water. When traveling, try ginger-root capsules from a pharmacy or health-food store. Another way to dock seasickness is to keep your vision fixed on the horizon. In a car, watch the road ahead of you, even if you're not driving.

☞ **Pain reliever.** There's now evidence that your instinct to rub where it hurts is for the good. When you stub your toe, for example, pain impulses rush up your leg to your spinal cord and to the brain. Rubbing the toe creates other impulses that interfere with the pain by taking up room along the same nerves. Here's how to rub a minor injury correctly:

1. Lightly move the skin in a circular motion with the pads of your fingertips.
2. If this feels comfortable, periodically intersperse long, flowing movements, gently pressing on the muscle. Pressing harder will not speed up the results.
3. Rub two or three times per day, about five minutes each time.
4. Never rub a serious injury, or an injury with broken skin, unless under a doctor's supervision.

☞ **Skin irritation.** For relief of the pain and itching caused by insect bites, mild cases of poison ivy, and sunburn, the low-maintenance aloe vera plant can be a godsend. When snapped in two, its succulent leaves release a balm that is instantly soothing to itchy skin. Aloe vera plants grow easily in sunny windows. Linseed oil is another all-purpose skin soother that relieves inflamed tissues and reduces itchiness.

☞ **Stiff muscles.** Before you pop a pill or buy a deep-heating liniment for stiff muscles or aching joints, try a sage bath. Wrap half a cup of dried sage in a piece of cheesecloth, then let it steep in a too-hot tub until the water reaches a comfortable level. A hot bath alone is soothing to both the mind and body, and sage is believed to increase these benefits.

☞ **Weight control.** If the problem is loss of appetite, then try munching on a few radishes before your next meal. The mustard oil in the flavorful root stimulates the desire to eat. On the other hand, if excessive weight is the problem, eat an apple to curb hunger and cut down on snacking. The magic ingredient is not fiber but pectin, which absorbs water in the stomach and makes you feel full.

☞ **Yeast infections.** Eat yogurt that contains live acidophilus cultures to prevent vaginal yeast infections. Medical tests are now demonstrating that this long-used folk remedy and prevention method is effective.

□ □ □

Saving at the Drugstore

There are several easy ways to save on high-priced prescription drugs, over-the-counter health products, and toiletries. First of all, always ask your doctor for small amounts of medications he or she recommends. Pharmaceutical companies are generous with the free samples they hand out to doctors to help promote their products, and doctors will pass them on when it makes sense.

Another way to save is to shop for medical prescriptions by phone or through the mail. Pharmail (800-237-8927), Medi-mail (800-331-1458), Action-Mail Order (800-452-1976), and Allscrips (800-972-7900) all offer drug discounts. Or shop at a local discount pharmacy chain like Duane Reade, Revco, or Eckerd's.

✍ **More by mail.** Retired Persons Services, Inc., the mail-order arm of the American Association of Retired Persons (AARP), sells prescription and non-prescription drugs, health and beauty aids, and more at big discounts. You do not have to be a member of AARP to order. Call the AARP pharmacy at 800-950-3909.

✍ **Keep it simple.** Beware of products that are overpackaged. They are wasteful and often cost more. For instance, buy toothpaste in old-fashioned tubes instead of pumps, and use a razor with disposable cartridges, not disposable razors.

✍ **Store brands.** Buy store brands or generic products instead of name brands. A close look at the ingredients on the label will usually tell you that corresponding store brands are very similar to national brands. Many discount stores offer store-brand alternatives to such products as Oil of Olay moisturizer and Neutrogena shampoo, to name just two. The chart on the next page compares name-brand items with store-brand ones. The store-brand savings on 20 products was 36%, for a total of $32.11.

Price Comparison of Name-Brand and Store-Brand Drugs

Item	Name-brand price	Store-brand price
Acetominophen, 100	$6.39	$3.84
Chest rub, 3 ounces	4.97	2.82
Cotton swabs, 300	1.69	1.45
Flouride toothpaste, 4 ounces	2.49	1.39
35mm film, 24 exposures	4.12	2.93
Hand/body lotion, 15 ounces	3.56	2.25
Liquid cold medicine, 10 ounces	6.85	4.23
Mint mouthwash, 24 ounces	4.08	2.36
Multivitamins, 100	8.85	5.93
Petroleum jelly, 13 ounces	3.24	2.34
Pink peptic bismuth, 8 ounces	3.25	2.35
Protein and balsam shampoo, 15 ounces	2.26	1.67
Roll-on deodorant, 2.5 ounces	3.28	2.03
Maxi sanitary napkins, 24 pads	3.00	2.56
Disposable twin razors, 10	3.90	2.24
Waxed dental floss, 100 yards	2.55	1.67
Ibuprofen, 100	7.90	5.41
Liquid cough suppressant, 8 ounces	5.54	2.98
Nasal spray, 1 ounce	6.94	3.09
Plastic first-aid strips, 50	2.73	1.94
Total	**$87.59**	**$55.48**

Source: Private Label Manufacturer's Association

Four Common Generics and What They Replace

Generic	Brand replaced	Savings
1. Ibuprofen (50 tablets, $2.59)	Advil (50 tablets, $5.59)	$3.00
2. Acetaminophen (100 tablets, $3.84)	Extra Strength Tylenol (100 tablets, $6.39)	$2.55
3. Antacid/antigas liquid (12 ounces, $2.79)	Maalox liquid (12 ounces, $4.99)	$2.20
4. Pseudoephedrine (24 tablets, $2.59)	Sudafed (24 tablets, $4.69)	$2.10

Don't!

☞ Do not spend money on **minoxidil** (brand name Rogaine), which has been shown to stimulate limited growth of hair, but only in men under 30 who have been balding for less than five years. Minoxidil must be used indefinitely (at between $50 and $100 a month) and may cause serious side effects.

☞ Do not take **laxatives**, which can cause a number of unpleasant side effects and can be addictive. Instead, eat plenty of fiber (prunes deserve their reputation) and drink at least eight glasses of fluids per day.

☞ Do not take **fish-oil supplements**. Although they have been advertised to prevent heart disease, the American Heart Association says this has not been proved. Two other good reasons not to take fish oil: It's fattening, and it can make you smell like fish.

☞ Do not buy **GH3**, also known as Gerovital, to cure arthritis, depression, hair loss, or other problems. It won't make you younger, as advertised—only poorer.

Beauty at a Fair Price

The cosmetics industry will try to convince you otherwise, but some of the best beautifiers are already right at your fingertips. You can often figure out cost-cutting alternatives to your favorite name-brand products by examining the ingredients and percentages listed on their packaging. Note the one or two ingredients that predominate. Then check to see if these are available in cheaper forms at the drugstore.

✔ **After-shave.** Make an after-shave lotion that's both refreshing and astringent by combining in a large glass jar one cup of witch-hazel extract, one tablespoon of cider vinegar, two tablespoons of dried sage, and two tablespoons of dried lavender flowers. Cover tightly and steep in bright sunlight for about a week. Shake periodically. Strain and bottle.

✔ **Astringent.** A good astringent or toner tightens pores and softens the skin. Make your own by combining a cup of crushed spearmint leaves and a pint of white vinegar in a glass jar. Cover tightly and steep in a sunny windowsill for a week. Shake periodically. Strain. Apply with cotton.

✔ **Bath oil.** Baby oil is an excellent stand-in for bath oil.

✔ **Cuticle cream.** Don't fall for cuticle creams, which have no special cuticle-mending properties. Rub petroleum jelly into your cuticles after bathing for hangnail-free hands. This also works for dry, scaly feet. Wear cotton socks after applying to feet.

✔ **Eye-makeup remover.** Don't buy eye-makeup remover; baby oil works just as well, even on waterproof mascara, and it won't irritate your eyes. Cetaphil lotion, which is reasonably priced and available at most drug and discount stores, is another good choice: It's non-irritating, fragrance-free, and greaseless.

✔ **Hair treatments.** Don't fall for "deep conditioning" hair treatments; nothing can actually penetrate the outer cuticle of the hair shaft. Care for your hair by eating right; crash diets are your hair's worst enemy. If you can't completely give up expensive hair-care products, replace just your shampoo with a less expensive supermarket brand while continuing to use your conditioner. To cut down on the need for conditioner, use an inexpensive wide-tooth comb to help end hair tangles. Run through wet hair after shampooing.

✔ **Tinted lip gloss.** Make your own by scooping out the last bit of lipstick in a tube with a cotton swab and combining it with petroleum jelly. Store in a pillbox or empty lip-balm container, and apply with a fingertip or lip brush.

✔ **Nail polish.** Store it in the refrigerator, and it will go on more smoothly and last longer. Don't let salespeople talk you into buying nail polish at the cosmetics counter; drugstore brands work just as well at half the price.

✔ **Nail-polish remover.** Buy plain acetone at the drugstore instead. It's the active ingredient minus the perfume. Hospitals use it to remove polish. And don't waste money on those saturated sponges that you dip your finger into; they're overpriced and don't stay clean long.

✔ **Skin cleaner.** Instead of buying commercial formulas, buy glycerin and lemon oil, both available at the drugstore. Mix a few drops of each together on your hands and rub in as you would hand lotion.

✔ **Teeth whiteners.** Simple baking soda is still one of the best ways to remove stains and brighten teeth. And it's a lot less expensive than commercial whiteners. Make a paste by combining a spoonful with a few drops of water, then brush with your toothbrush for one minute. Repeat as often as you like, ideally once each week.

Bargain Beauty Buys Through the Mail

When you just have to have a certain name-brand product, check out the free catalogs from these two reputable wholesalers:
Beautiful Visions (516-567-0990) and Beauty Boutique (Box 94520, 6836 Engle Road, Cleveland, OH 44101-4520; 216-826-3008). They both offer savings of up to 90% and accept returns.

Back to Basics With Skin Care

Claiming solutions for everything from enlarged pores to the aging process, new skin-care products vie for attention like boxing promoters. But in this game there's no knockout punch. Don't let anybody tell you that a product can "nourish" your skin with vitamins, herbs, or any other magical panaceas. The only way to nourish the skin is through a balanced diet. Likewise, the best way to hydrate the skin is by drinking plenty of water (at least eight glasses a day, more during hot weather and after exercise). Moisturizer only helps to hold in what's already there.

Any expert will tell you that the most important thing you can do for your skin is to stay out of the sun. Scarves, hats, and sunglasses are effective protectors, and they never run dry. In addition, a back-to-basics skin-care routine is your best bet. Get off the spending cycle of empty promises and back on the road to clean, healthy good looks. Here are some cost-cutter tips that come with the hearty approval of dermatologists:

Don't disturb your face any more than is necessary. Use a mild, unscented soap on your face no more than twice a day. If your skin is dry, rinse your face with tepid water in the morning and clean it with a glycerin-based (clear) soap at night. Finish with a splash of cold water, the best way to shrink large pores.

For dry skin, try a cream cleanser. If even mild soap leaves your skin dry and irritated, use a cream cleanser, but not a fancy cosmetics-counter brand. Many female dermatologists say they use Pond's cold cream as a cleanser in their skin-care regimens.

Use a light moisturizer with a built-in sunscreen. It saves money because you get two products in one. Again, stick to the discount drugstore; plenty of effective products are available. Just be sure to buy a lotion with a Sun Protection Factor (SPF) of 15 or higher. Since any product claiming an SPF of 15 or more must adhere to FDA guidelines, you can be assured of quality. Paying extra means perfume, packaging, and prestige, none of which prevents wrinkles.

Get a good, stiff washcloth. Expensive exfoliants, which are simply gritty creams (sometimes the grit is something exotic), are no more effective than a cheap washcloth. Skin-care experts sometimes confess to scouring discount stores for the lowest-quality washcloths they can find—the cheaper the cloth, the rougher the wash.

□ □ □

Gain While You Lose
Nutritional Bargains for Cost-Effective Dieting

No magic secrets will help you achieve and maintain an ideal weight. No pills, powders, or radical diets will work. We've all heard by now what we need to do: Eat moderate amounts of low-fat, nutritious foods and burn more calories than we take in by exercising regularly. Expensive diet programs and health spas help some people, but don't let anyone tell you that you can't make changes on your own.

A good rule of thumb is to shop for "whole" foods, or foods that haven't been altered too much since they came out of the ground. For example, whole-wheat flour contains the entire grain, while white flour has been stripped of its valuable outer layers, including the bran and the germ. An apple is a better snack choice than a glass of apple juice, which contains the sugar of four or five apples and none of the beneficial (and filling) fiber. Here are some cost-conscious diet tips to get you on your way:

✔ **Eat water-based soups to start meals.** They fill the stomach and curtail appetite with few calories. Make your own cheap and tasty pot by starting with beef or chicken broth and adding saved-up leftover vegetables.

✔ **The much-maligned potato is a dieter's pal, and it's cheap.** A potato is virtually fat-free, low in sodium, and filling while being light in calories: A five-ounce spud weighs in at a mere 100. Potatoes are also packed with vitamins, minerals, and fiber, especially in the skin. Watch out for the fat that usually accompanies potatoes, though. Try topping a baked potato with plain yogurt blended with chives, or sprinkle on some part-skim mozzarella and herbs during the last five minutes of baking.

✔ **Avoid frozen "diet entrées."** While the calorie counts on these overpriced, undersize products seem low, a high percentage of those calories are often fatty. For the same serving-control benefits, and to add fiber and reduce fat and sodium, freeze your own dinners ahead of time in single-serving containers.

✔ **Skip processed lunch meats.** Ham, salami, bologna, and liverwurst, which cost from $3.99 to $6.99 per pound, are sky-high in sodium, and derive up to 90% of their calories from fat. To pack healthier, cheaper lunches, cook a bigger chicken or turkey (about $3 per pound) than you'll need for dinner and thinly slice leftovers for sandwiches. Also try reduced-cholesterol egg salad by removing all but a few yolks before chopping, then dress with reduced-fat mayonnaise or a mixture of low-fat yogurt and Dijon mustard.

✔ **Buy a hot-air popcorn popper.** It will quickly pay for itself by cutting down snack-food costs and dramatically reducing fat and calories. Minus the oil and butter, air-popped corn contains just 23 calories per cup, plus more fiber than a slice of whole-wheat bread. So even a late-night binge can be guilt-free. Try topping popcorn with crushed herbs or salt-free table seasoning instead of salt.

✔ **Ice-cream alternatives.** Try fat-free fruit ices and sorbets for dessert instead of ice cream, which usually contains more than 10% cholesterol-laden butterfat. Those expensive brands in small containers can deliver more than 20% fat and a whopping 1,200 calories per pint. If you have a food processor, make your own healthy fruit sherbet by blending together two cups of frozen strawberries or raspberries, 3/4 cup of skim milk, and a few teaspoons of sugar, honey, or frozen juice concentrate, to taste.

☐ ☐ ☐

Health Insurance: Getting the Most for Your Money

As many as 60 million Americans are considered to be inadequately insured. Nobody likes to spend a lot on insurance; it's one of those things you don't appreciate until you need it. But rest assured, the money you invest in a sound health-insurance policy is well spent. You might not want to be covered for the dings and the scratches, but you certainly want to be covered for a major accident. This potentially huge out-of-pocket expense can be devastating, and it's really the reason why we buy insurance.

The trick is to find the policy that fits your needs best, providing the maximum amount of coverage for the least cost. Once you have settled on a policy, be sure to know the rules so you can minimize your out-of-pocket expenses. Health-care costs are rising rapidly, but you can help keep them in check. Here's how:

✔ **Check out group policies.** Many trade and professional associations offer their members group insurance, including major medical, disability, long-term care, and life insurance. These group policies may be less expensive than individual policies.

✔ **Don't buy cancer insurance.** It's not a good idea to buy disease-specific policies, such as cancer insurance. What you need is a comprehensive health-care insurance plan, not a policy that protects only against specific illnesses under specific conditions.

✔ **Shop for price.** Many people ask, Why should I shop for lower prices if my insurance company pays the bill? Two reasons: It helps control insurance-coverage costs, which you pay, and it lowers your deductible or co-payment. Most insurance companies pay only a portion of your total medical bill. The lower your total bill, the lower your share of the bill.

✔ **Customary and reasonable fees.** Let's say your insurance policy covers 100% of your doctor's fees. That means you don't need to worry about what the doctor is charging, right? Wrong. In insurance policies, 100% often means 100% of "usual, customary, and reasonable" fees. To make sure you don't get charged the difference between what your doctor feels is reasonable and what your insurance company feels is reasonable, determine what the costs will be beforehand and check them with your insurance company.

✔ **Buy generic drugs.** Many insurance companies pay 100% for generic drugs, but only 80% for name-brand drugs. Ask your doctor to prescribe a generic whenever possible. If your doctor forgets, check with the pharmacist. In many states, they are allowed to make the substitution themselves unless the physician marks "dispense as written" on the prescription. For a copy of *The Smart Consumer's Guide to Prescription Drugs* (No. D13579), contact the American Association of Retired Persons (Attention: Consumer Affairs, 601 E Street, NW, Washington, DC 20049; 202-434-6031).

✔ **File claims ASAP.** Some insurance policies won't pay claims filed six months after treatment.

✔ **Follow the rules.** Many insurance companies require a "second opinion" or "pre-admission review" before they will pay for surgery. Unless it is emergency surgery, many companies penalize you or refuse to pay if you don't get a second opinion. Know the rules of your policy. Most companies pay for the second opinion.

✔ **Stake your claim.** If you have long waits for reimbursement or claims you think were wrongly rejected, fight back. About half the states require health insurers to pay claims within a specified number of days, typically 30 or 45. First, call your insurance company's customer-service department and complain. If you aren't satisfied, call your state insurance commissioner's office.

✔ **Health-club rebates.** Many insurers are offering rebates to policyholders who join health clubs and demonstrate regular attendance. U.S. Healthcare, for example, gives $200 a year if you provide a letter from the health club.

Is an HMO the Answer?

In response to rising health-care costs in the 1970s and 1980s, new "managed care" health-care delivery systems appeared on the scene. These arrangements—known as health maintenance organizations (HMOs), preferred provider organizations (PPOs), exclusive provider organizations (EPOs), point-of-service (POS) plans, and independent practice associations (IPAs), among others—try to keep costs down by creating networks of health-care providers.

Under the managed-care system, you pay a monthly membership fee, and the system pays your medical bills. You can usually join an HMO through your employer, but you might also be able to join through open enrollment. These organizations work on the principle that an ounce of prevention is worth a pound of cure. **HMOs encourage you to go to the doctor**—in some cases charging as little as $2 a visit. (Most normal insurance plans don't cover checkups.) If you join an HMO, **take advantage of the preventive-care services they offer**, such as well-baby visits, immunizations, and annual physical exams.

The booklet *HMOs: Are They Right for You?* summarizes the advantages and disadvantages of choosing an HMO. For a copy send $3.85 to the American Council on Science and Health (1995 Broadway, 2nd Floor, New York, NY 10023-5860; 212-362-7044).

For free copies of *More Health for Your Dollar: An Older Person's Guide to HMOs* (No. D1195) and *Choosing an HMO: An Evaluation Checklist* (No. D12444), contact the AARP, 202-434-6031.

✔ **For more health-insurance information.** For free information, write to the Health Insurance Association of America (1025 Connecticut Avenue, NW, Suite 1200, Washington, DC 20036; 202-223-7780).

✔ **Medicare supplement insurance.** The government's Medicare insurance program for people over age 65 pays only about 45% of health-care expenses. It's up to the enrollee to come up with the difference. In response, many insurance companies offer "Medigap" policies—supplemental insurance designed to fill holes in Medicare's coverage. When shopping for a Medigap policy, look carefully at what the policy says about any health problems you have now or have had in the past. Pre-existing conditions usually aren't covered until a specific period of time has elapsed. Also consider HMO coverage; it might be cheaper than a good Medicare supplement insurance policy. *Note:* Don't buy a Medigap policy if you qualify for Medicaid, which pays all your bills. And don't buy more than one policy. Money spent this way is usually wasted because coverage overlaps.

For a free copy of the National Association of Insurance Commissioners' *Guide to Health Insurance for People With Medicare*, contact the NAIC (Publications Department, 120 W. 12th Street, Suite 1100, Kansas City, MO 64105; 816-842-3600). The brochure *Medicare: What It Covers, What It Doesn't* (No. D13133) is free from the AARP, 202-434-2230.

For a copy of *A Consumer's Guide to Health Insurance* or *A Consumer's Guide to Medicare Supplement Insurance*, contact Health Insurance Association of America (Box 41455, Washington, DC 20018).

✔ **Disability insurance.** Health insurance is only part of the story. Disability insurance provides you with an income should you become sick or injured and unable to work. Many people overlook the importance of this insurance. But if you are between the ages of 35 and 65, your chances of being unable to work for 90 days or more because of a disabling illness or injury are about equal to your chances of dying.

Most salaried workers participate in the Social Security program, which includes disability benefits. Your salary and the number of years you have been covered under Social Security determine how much you receive. You might also receive benefits through your employer.

Because disability benefits are generally tax-free, you need to insure yourself for only up to 75% of your current wages, including Social Security disability and other benefits. When assessing insurance needs, consider the way the policy defines disability. Some policies—including the Social Security disability program—define disability as the inability to perform any gainful employment, not the inability to do the job you were doing at the time of injury.

Remember, you're insuring against long-term disability, not short-term illness. Reduce your premiums by up to 50% by lengthening the waiting period—the time between the beginning of your disability and when benefits kick in—from 30 to 90 days. But don't skimp on the benefit period; you want to be covered until you are 65. And do take inflation protection. It's crucial to maintaining your standard of living should you become disabled.

For a free copy of *The Consumer's Guide to Disability Insurance*, contact the Health Insurance Association of America (Box 41455, Washington, DC 20018).

Long-Term Care Insurance

Medicare pays for very little of the extended day-in, day-out care that many older people need, and these long-term care expenses can add up fast: a year in a nursing home costs on average between $25,000 and $30,000. You need to be covered for this, but one way to cut down on your insurance premiums is to choose a long waiting period (up to 100 days) before the insurance kicks in.

It's best to be well informed on this subject if it looks like you or a relative will be in need of this service soon. For a copy of *A Consumer's Guide to Long-Term Care Insurance*, contact the Health Insurance Association of America (Box 41455, Washington, DC 20018). For a catalog of information and brochures on long-term care and other health-care issues, contact the American Health Care Association (Publications, Dept. L, Box 96906, Washington, DC 20090-6906; 800-321-0343).

For a copy of the Better Business Bureau's *Long-Term Nursing Home Care* brochure, send $1 and a self-addressed, stamped envelope to the Better Business Bureau (Dept. 023, Washington, DC 20042-0023) and request publication No. 07-24-248. For copies of *The Consumer's Guide to Life-Care Communities*, or *The Consumer's Guide to Home Health Care*, send $4 to the National Consumers League (Suite 928-N, 815 15th Street, NW, Washington, DC 20005; 202-639-8140).

□ □ □

Chapter 8

Money Management

Savings in this chapter...

During the past decade, the world of personal finance has grown increasingly complex. You can't depend on your local bank to meet all your financial needs anymore. Simple checking accounts have been replaced by interest-earning NOW accounts and money-market checking accounts. The once ubiquitous passbook savings account is now considered one step above a piggy bank. Instead, certificates of deposit, Treasury securities, EE bonds, mutual funds, and countless other savings and investment options should be considered.

Your financial security depends on more than just how you save money. You might be squandering tens of thousands of dollars through bad loan choices. The difference of just one percentage point on a $100,000, 30-year mortgage totals almost $27,000 over the life of the loan. Is it time for you to refinance your mortgage? See page 143. The credit cards you carry can also cost—or save—you money on a monthly basis. If your wallet is stuffed with high-interest credit cards and all you can afford to pay is the monthly minimum, you're losing money that could be spent much more wisely. You need to learn how to make your cards work for you (page 138), not the other way around.

A secure financial plan also includes adequate insurance. Do you have enough life insurance to provide for your family when you die? Is your home protected against loss from fire, theft, and natural disaster? The appropriate policies can help you and your family face the future without fear of financial ruin.

Though many people seek the counsel of experienced financial planners, you don't need to be a *Wall Street Journal* junkie to save—and make—money. But you do need to follow the rules of frugality described in this chapter when making some tough financial decisions.

□ □ □

Getting the Most From Your Checking Account

To get the most out of your banking dollar, carefully consider your checking-account options. If you can afford the minimum balance requirements, the best accounts are typically interest-bearing NOW accounts or credit-union share-draft accounts. Select an account with the lowest minimum (or average) balance that allows you to earn interest and avoid fees. Don't leave surplus cash in your checking account, even if it does earn interest. (Money market accounts and other investments offer higher rates.) The best accounts—and, fortunately, the most common—are day-of-deposit-to-day-of-withdrawal accounts, which pay interest from the day you put money in the bank to the day you take it out. Here are some other ways to make sure your checking account isn't costing you needlessly:

$ Compare monthly service and transaction fees. You can save $100 or more per year by choosing a bank with low fees. Take into consideration bounced-check charges, which can cost up to $30 at some institutions.

$ Choose direct deposit. When possible, have checks deposited directly into your account. Your money begins earning interest sooner this way than if you wait for checks to arrive and take them to the bank yourself.

$ Pay less for checks. Theoretically you could write a check on a spare door if you could mail it. In any case, you don't need to pay your bank premium rates for their blank checks. Instead, order them directly from a printer. Current (800-426-0822) and Checks in the Mail (800-733-4443) both charge $4.95 for the first 200 checks and $6.95 for every 200 thereafter—about 50% less than most banks.

$ Know when you expect checks for deposit. More than 1.4 million government checks—over half of which are Social Security payments—are lost or stolen each year. If you expect a government check that doesn't arrive on time, wait three days, then notify the Social Security Administration at 800-772-1213.

□ □ □

Credit Cards: How to Choose 'Em, How to Use 'Em

Ever try to rent a car without a credit card? It's usually more trouble than it's worth. Today, credit and charge cards make traveling, shopping by phone, donating to charity—indeed, most activities involving money—a lot easier. The key is to use the cards to *your* advantage, not the bank's. Here's how:

$ Know thy card. It's important to understand the difference between charge and credit cards. A charge card, such as American Express or Diners Club, is basically just a convenient way of paying for your purchases. You're not extended any credit and are expected to pay your balance in full each month. Your only cost is the annual fee and prohibitive interest payments if you do happen to pay late.

Using a credit card, such as Visa or MasterCard, is really taking out a small loan to pay for purchases. The bank determines your credit-worthiness and assigns you a credit line, which determines how much money you can borrow at a time. Your loan is interest-free for the first month, but after that you pay interest, usually at an annual rate somewhere between 12% and 20%. You also generally pay an annual fee. The best way to use credit cards is to treat them like charge cards. That means you shouldn't charge anything you can't pay for at the end of the month. Of course, for a major purchase, you might have to make an exception, but you should pay it off as quickly as possible. The longer you take to pay for it, the more it costs you.

$ Cut back on your cards. Most couples don't need more than two cards. The ideal mix is one credit card (Visa and MasterCard are the most widely accepted) and one charge card (American Express or Diners Club). Then let each spouse be the primary cardholder for one and the supplemental cardholder (piggybacking on the other's account) for the other. That way you pay only one full fee plus one reduced fee for each card, and each of you keeps records for and pays only one bill.

$ Keep it separate. If you own a business, it's worthwhile to spend the extra money on another credit or charge card. Use that one just for business, and then you won't spend extra time separating expenses come tax season.

$ Choosing a credit card. Shop around for the best terms just as you would for a mortgage or car loan. Each bank sets its own annual fees, interest rates, finance and late charges, and so forth. If you regularly pay your balance in full and on time, as you should, look for a card that provides a grace period, limits transaction charges, and has a low annual fee. If you don't pay your bill in full each month, look for a card with a low interest rate, too.

For help in deciding among the approximately 6,000 U.S. banks that offer Visa and MasterCard, contact Bankcard Holders of America (560 Herndon Parkway, Suite 120, Herndon, VA 22070; 800-553-8025). For $4 this nonprofit consumer credit education and advocacy organization will send you a list of banks that offer low interest rates and no annual fee.

$ Pay your bills on time. Prompt payment is in your interest. Not only does it save you finance charges, but many credit-card issuers reward good customers with lower interest rates. The Optima Card, for instance, charges only 12.5% interest if you've had your card for at least a year, charged a minimum of $1,000 on it, and always paid your bill on time. If you meet the last requirement but not the first two, you pay a rate of 14.75%, but if you've had a late payment, you get stuck with an 18.75% rate.

$ Lost or stolen card. Report it as soon as possible—on the 24-hour hotline. If charges have been made before you report it missing, you'll have to cover the first $50.

$ Correct errors quickly. If you find a mistake on your billing statement, respond quickly and in writing. The Fair Credit Billing Act states that you must report a disputed charge to the card issuer in writing within 60 days of the date postmarked on the billing statement. The issuer must also inform you in writing that it is investigating or has solved the problem within 30 days of receiving your letter and must correct the error or send you a written explanation within 90 days. You are not required to pay the charge in question until the dispute has been settled (but the issuer is allowed to freeze that amount against your credit line).

$ Reap the rewards. Many credit and charge cards now have tie-ins with airlines to provide frequent-flier miles for every dollar you charge on your card. These programs are well worth the annual fee (usually around $25) if you charge enough each year to receive a free ticket or two.

$ Take advantage of free benefits. Many people fail to take advantage of some of the best features of their cards—free benefits. Check the list of services your card issuer provides. American Express cardmembers, for instance, are entitled to the following free programs:

✔ The Purchase Protection Plan automatically insures most purchases against accidental damage and theft for up to 90 days and up to $1,000. (For details, call American Express at 800-322-1277).

✔ The Buyer's Assurance Protection Plan doubles the free repair period of the manufacturer's warranty—up to an additional year—for many products. (Call 800-225-3750.)

✔ The Lemon Assurance Program prevents you from getting stuck with products that keep breaking down. If you have a product repaired and it still fails to work, you can get it replaced through the program at no charge. (Call 800- 322-1277.)

✔ You automatically receive $100,000 in Travel Accident Insurance any time you charge your tickets with the American Express Card. (Call 800-THE-CARD.)

✔ Privileges on Call is a hotline that cardmembers can use to find out about special offers—discounted airfares, rental cars, lodging, meals, entertainment, etc.—available only to them. (Call 800-835-5000.)

These are just some of the free programs that American Express offers, and many other cards provide similar services. Read your card brochures and newsletters or call your cards' customer representatives for more information.

$ Pay card debt first. When reducing your debt, the first thing you should do is to pay off your credit cards. It's foolish to roll over debt at 16% or 18% annual interest. And remember, you can no longer deduct interest payments from your taxes.

Using Credit and Charge Cards Wisely

Never charge any item under $25. A significant amount of unneeded debt stems from small purchases that probably wouldn't have been made if the person had a policy of only paying cash for small purchases.

Don't go for the gold. Unless a premium card offers special services you need, skip it. Most charge higher annual fees.

Know your rights. The government publishes booklets on consumer credit, the Fair Credit Reporting Act, and other consumer topics. For a list of these titles, request a copy of the *Consumer Information Catalog* from the Consumer Information Center (Box 100, Pueblo, CO 81002).

Avoid credit-card cash advances. Most credit cards charge a fee ($2 to $3 or a surcharge of up to 5%) for cash advances—and they charge interest from the day you get your hands on the money. Instead of taking cash from a credit card, withdraw the money from your checking or savings account. If the money isn't available, you probably can't afford to spend it.

Ask merchants for cash discounts. When they agree, pocket your card. Many merchants, especially small ones, give discounts of 5% to 10% on cash purchases.

Say no to affinity accounts. Don't sign up for affinity cards, which are supposed to support the sponsoring charity, educational institution, or nonprofit organization. In most cases the group receives a very small slice of the pie—and you pay more than you need to for the card. Instead, shop for the best deal on a credit card and write a check to your charity. That way your contribution is tax-deductible, too.

Where to Find Cheap Loans

Almost everyone borrows money at some point in his or her life—to buy a house, go to college, or get behind the wheel. Save significant amounts of money—tens of thousands of dollars over the lifetime of your loan—by carefully shopping for the right terms at the right price.

Many financial problems start with the unwise use of credit. Excluding mortgage payments, loans should not take up more than 20% of your take-home pay. If you're drowning in debt, you must slow down your spending. Don't depend on a consolidation loan to ease the load. You'll ultimately pay more in interest if you stretch out the payments, and four out of five people who take out consolidation loans replace their monthly debt load within two years. You must develop a budget—and be disciplined enough to stick to it.

Don't seek out more credit than you need. Though few people realize it, unused credit is often counted against you when you seek a loan. You don't want to be turned down for a home mortgage or a car loan because your credit report shows a dozen credit cards, each with significant limits. Even if you never use the card, high credit limits can compromise your creditworthiness. As far as the bank is concerned, at any minute you could go out and charge purchases left and right, until you're overextended.

Borrow from yourself. If you have a retirement plan and it has a loan provision, you may be allowed to borrow money for certain purposes. You might not have to pay taxes or penalties as long as you repay the loan within five years. And because the interest is paid to your account, the loan is virtually free. Compare that with a personal loan or a line of credit at your bank for which you may pay 10% to 21% interest.

Consider joining a credit union. Credit unions are nonprofit financial co-ops that provide members financial services. They often offer loans at cheaper rates than banks and other institutions. About half of all Americans belong to groups with credit unions. For a list of unions run by organizations you might belong to, contact the National Credit Union Administration (202-682-9600) and ask for your regional office.

Negotiate the right mortgage. Don't assume that interest rates and points are etched in stone. Shop around, and ask lenders whether there is any flexibility in the rates. You can also save a lot of money by paying off your mortgage early. One option is to take out a 30-year loan and pay it off as if it were a 15-year loan by making additional payments on the principal each month. You get the benefits of the shorter-term loan, but if you ever become financially squeezed, you can make the smaller monthly payment due on the 30-year loan.

The savings can be significant. Say you took out a $100,000 mortgage for 30 years at 10.5% interest. Your monthly payments would be $915. If you increased your payments by $25 a month, you'd pay off your mortgage in about 25 years—and you'd save more than $40,000 in interest. If you paid $50 more each month, you'd save $66,000. If you paid $100 more, you'd pocket an extra $98,000 and own your house outright in just 19 years.

If interest rates are on a roller coaster when you apply for a mortgage, consider a mortgage lock-in. This provision freezes the interest rate and points applicable at the time you apply. Lock-ins ensure that what you shop for is what you get. There may be a fee for locking in the rate—either a flat fee, a percentage of the mortgage amount, or a fraction of a percentage point added to the rate you lock in. But remember, lock-ins can work for or against you. If rates go down between the time you apply for a mortgage and the time it is approved, you may not be able to take advantage of the lower rates. For a free copy of *A Consumer's Guide to Mortgage Lock-ins*, contact the Board of Governors of the Federal Reserve System (Publications Services, Mailstop No. 138, Washington, DC 20551; 202-452-3245).

If you have an adjustable-rate mortgage, check the math. As many as one in three ARMs is calculated wrong. If you need help with the calculations, contact HSH Associates (Department ACK, 1200 Route 23, Butler, NJ 07405-2015; 800-873-2837) and ask for the $3 ARM Check Kit. HSH also offers Refinancing and Home-Equity Kits for $3.

□ □ □

When to Refinance Your Mortgage

Refinancing your mortgage allows you to trade in a high interest rate for a lower one. Then, because you'll have "extra" cash from the transaction, you can either reduce your monthly payments or pay off your mortgage faster.

If you bought a house when mortgage interest rates were low, you have no need to refinance. But if you bought your home when rates were higher or if you have an adjustable-rate loan and want to convert to a low-interest, fixed-rate loan, you may want to consider refinancing your mortgage.

A general rule of thumb is that refinancing becomes worthwhile if the current interest rate on your mortgage is at least two percentage points higher than the prevailing market rate. This minimum spread is required in order to meet the refinancing costs. You should also consider how long you plan to stay in the house. It usually takes at least three years to make up for the costs of refinancing, because you have to pay an application fee, a title search, title insurance, the lender's attorney's fees, loan-origination fees and points, appraisal fees, and any prepayment penalties. In most cases, these expenses total an average of 3% to 6% of the outstanding principal. But there are ways to cut costs.

Ask the company that sold you your title insurance whether it can reissue your policy at a "reissue rate." You should save up to 70% of what it would cost for a new policy.

For a free copy of *A Consumer's Guide to Mortgage Refinancing*, contact the Board of Governors of the Federal Reserve System (Publications Services, Mailstop No. 138, Washington, DC 20551; 202-452-3245).

□ □ □

Saving and Investing

We can't overemphasize the importance of setting aside a sum of money—any sum—on a regular basis. It's no longer practical to count on the value of your house to automatically increase enough to fund your children's college educations and your retirement. You're going to have to save hard cash.

Your initial goal should be at least six months' salary in a liquid account—one that can easily be converted to cash. To achieve that goal, you should get in the habit of saving a portion of your income every payday. You can begin by socking away as little as 1% or 2% of your income, but gradually increase that to at least 10%. Once you recognize the importance of saving, it's easy to make it a part of your life.

Six Steps to Bigger Savings

1. Make a check out to your savings account. Rearrange your thinking so that saving becomes one of your expenses, as crucial as the rent or mortgage payment. If you allow saving to be what comes after you've taken care of paying all your other bills, then the money will slip through your fingers. Saving is an integral part of your household budget. Make a check out to your savings account every month when you pay bills.

2. Set goals. Set short- and long-term financial goals and save for specific expenses. Most people save for education and retirement, but you should also have a fund for a new car, your next vacation, a swimming pool, or whatever you're aiming for. Also, decide how much time you have to reach your goals. Obviously, retirement is a long-term goal, but your next vacation may require only a year of saving.

Having various funds makes saving more fun, and it reminds you that you're setting aside money for the purpose of enriching your life—not just to amass cash.

3. Arrange to have your savings deposited automatically. If you can, sign up for an employer-sponsored salary-reduction plan like a 401(k) or 403(b). These plans save money because the contributions reduce your current taxable income, and the interest, dividends, and capital gains are tax-sheltered until you withdraw your money or retire. Most plans automatically invest for you each payday, and many employers match some or all of what you put in. If your company doesn't offer a savings plan that can be automatically deducted from your monthly paycheck, work with your bank to electronically transfer funds on a regular basis from your checking to your savings account.

Buying treasury securities. For information on how to buy Treasury securities at no charge, call the Bureau of the Public Debt, Public Information Center (202-874-4000). You can also buy Treasury securities from any Federal Reserve Bank.

---

4. It's never too early to start saving for retirement. If at age 21 you begin investing $2,000 a year for 10 years in an individual retirement account earning 9% interest, you'll have $620,000 by age 65—without contributing a dime to the account after age 30. If you wait 10 years to start contributing and continue to age 65, your nest egg will contain $189,000 less. Consider starting with an individual retirement account. IRAs, the most familiar tax-deferred accounts, aren't the final word in retirement planning—your contributions are relatively small and your annual contribution is tax-deductible only if you're not covered by a company pension plan—but they are a good start.

5. Keogh if you can. Keoghs (named after the congressman who sponsored the enacting legislation) are retirement plans for the self-employed and for people with an income-producing business outside their regular employment. Like IRAs, Keoghs are tax-deferred, but unlike IRAs, they are deductible for everyone, regardless of income level or coverage by another pension plan. You can contribute and deduct from current taxes up to $30,000 or 15% of your income (whichever is lower) per year in a Keogh plan, but because they are somewhat complicated to set up and operate, use an IRA account if your planned annual contributions aren't more than $2,000.

Investing Wisely

Don't even think about investing until you've reached your savings goal of six months' salary. You don't want to have money in stocks, bonds, or anything else that fluctuates in value until you have a pool of money to draw on for daily living—and for emergencies. You never know when your roof is going to leak or your car is going to need a new transmission. Do you have enough insurance? You should have adequate life, health, disability, and homeowner's insurance before you call a broker or financial adviser.

When considering investments, keep in mind that interest rates alone don't mean much. The key to making money is the difference between interest rates and inflation. It's better to earn a 5% return when inflation is 4% than to earn 12% when inflation is 13%.

Seek competent help. Before selecting a financial adviser, talk to at least three prospective planners. Ask about their background, experience, registration—and how they are compensated. Be aware that brokers and many financial planners earn a commission on the products they sell. In some cases, brokers have an incentive to sell certain stocks that the firm owns, and you might be able to get discounts of 20% to 30% on the commission. Ask.

Play it safe—sometimes. Choose some secure short-term investments, such as certificates of deposit or government bonds. These low-risk investments don't promise amazing returns, but they provide safe, steady income. Buy certificates of deposit from federally insured institutions. The Federal Deposit Insurance Corporation (FDIC) and the Federal Savings and Loan Insurance Corporation (FSLIC) insure deposits for up to $100,000 per account. For the latest market-based rate information on U.S. bonds, call 800-4US-BOND or 800-US-BONDS. You don't have to pay state or local taxes on government EE bonds. And if you use the bonds to pay for educational expenses for yourself, your spouse, or your child, you may be able to avoid federal taxes, too. Your right to tax-exemption depends on your modified adjusted gross income. For details, request publication SBD-1964 from the Office of Public Affairs (U.S. Savings

Bond Division, Washington, DC 20226).

Take chances—sometimes. If you're investing long-term—15 to 20 years—consider putting your money in the stock market or in stock mutual funds. Look for a reasonable balance of risk and growth. And keep in mind the following pointers:

☞ **Think long-term.** Don't go after the hot mutual fund of the month. Always evaluate the five- or 10-year record of a fund, because that will encompass both up and down markets.

☞ **Avoid odd lots.** You'll pay more to buy and sell in irregular blocks.

☞ **Sign up for dividend-reinvestment plans.** Many corporations allow you to invest your dividends in the purchase of additional shares of stock. In many cases you can avoid service fees and broker commissions by opting for such reinvestment plans.

Never buy an investment you don't understand. Don't be afraid to ask questions. Legitimate companies want you to know the answers. For a free copy of the booklet *Investment Swindles: How They Work and How to Avoid Them*, contact the National Futures Association (Attention: Public Affairs Department, 200 West Madison Street, Suite 1600, Chicago, IL 60606-3447; 800-621-3570, 800-572-9400 in Illinois).

□ □ □

How to Cut Your Taxes

Those who save the most on taxes plan ahead and watch out for tax breaks all year round. It's too late to begin thinking of tax-saving strategies on April 14. Your local community college probably offers an adult-education tax course at night; the $10 or so you'll pay for a session is money well spent. In the meantime, these tips can help you begin planning taxes for the coming year:

$ Give till it hurts. Clean out your house and hold a garage sale. Everything you can't sell, give away and take a tax deduction on. But be aware that the IRS keeps a watchful eye on charitable contributions. For noncash contributions of more than $500 but not more than $5,000, you must attach an additional form to your return. For noncash contributions of more than $5,000, you're required to obtain an independent appraisal of the property. For details on claiming deductions for charitable donations, call the IRS at 800-829-3676 and request IRS Publication 561, *Determining the Value of Donated Property*.

$ Write a check to charity. When making charitable contributions, always pay by check or credit card so that you'll have a record. If you do use cash, ask for a receipt. If you're asked to buy candy, cards, or tickets to an event, only the portion of the payment that the charity keeps is tax-deductible. For example, if you spend $100 on a charity dinner and the dinner costs the charity $25, then you can deduct $75.

$ Fight your property-tax appraisal. With home values dropping in many parts of the country, your town or county has to justify rising assessments.

$ Keep your home-improvement receipts. When you remodel or improve your home, keep all receipts in a safe place. These costs increase your basis in the home and reduce taxable gains when you sell, but you must have accurate records of your expenses.

$ Claim every dependent. If you and other family members are supporting a parent or other relative who has medical expenses, decide early in the year who will claim the dependent. To deduct the dependent's medical expenses, you must pay the bills and claim the dependent on your return. If you and your siblings jointly support a parent but none of you pays more than half the support, you can file a multiple support agreement (IRS Form 2120) to get a dependency exemption that can be assigned to one of you.

$ Pay state and local taxes early. If you pay state and local estimated income taxes by December 31, you can claim a deduction for them on this year's federal tax return.

$ Fully fund your retirement plan. The wages you put into retirement plans are not currently taxable, up to certain limits.

$ Review your withholding. The amount of your income-tax withholding and estimated payments should be high enough to avoid underpayment penalties, but low enough to avoid lending your money to Uncle Sam for a year without interest.

$ Don't twiddle your thumbs. When dealing with the Internal Revenue Service, respond promptly to all correspondence. If you delay, you could incur steep penalties and interest charges. For free copies of IRS publications and forms, call 800-829-3676. Ask for Publication 17,

Your Federal Income Tax, and Publication 910, *Guide to Free Tax Services*, for an overview of the assistance that is available.

□ □ □

Choosing the Right Insurance Policies

While most people find shopping for insurance an unpleasant experience—who wants to think about potential misfortune and disaster?—buying adequate insurance is the only way to protect yourself and your family from financial ruin in case of catastrophe. You can save money on most policies by paying your insurance bills annually instead of monthly and avoiding service fees and interest penalties. For general information on auto, health, homeowner's, disability, or life insurance, call the National Insurance Consumer Helpline (800-942-4242), which is sponsored by the insurance-industry trade associations.

Life Insurance

When buying life insurance, remember it's not for you—it's for the people you leave behind. If you don't have kids and your spouse has high earning power, you might not need a policy at all.

There are two main types of life insurance—term and cash-value. A term policy provides coverage for a specified term, usually one, five, 10, or 20 years. It pays a benefit only if the insured dies during the time the policy is in effect. The premiums for term insurance are low in the early years, when the need is greatest, and higher in later years, when insurance needs decline. As the premiums rise, reassess your needs and lower the amount of coverage. Cash-value insurance is more expensive at first, but the payments don't increase as you grow older. These policies gradually build cash value; they are in essence a long-term savings plan. If you cancel the policy, you can receive the cash value. You can also borrow against it.

In general, you buy more insurance protection for less money by choosing term insurance, but you don't build equity. Consider buying term insurance and taking the difference between the annual premium for a cash-value policy and the annual premium for a term policy and investing that money yourself. In essence, you would be creating your own cash-value insurance program—only you must be disciplined enough to stick by your plan. Here are some life-insurance tips:

$ Buy a renewable policy. Renewable term insurance is somewhat more expensive—about 25¢ to 60¢ per $1,000 of coverage—but it's worth it. With such a policy, the company must renew your insurance at your request unless you haven't paid your premium.

$ Ask about discounts. Does the insurer offer lower premiums for nonsmokers or for people who attend exercise classes regularly?

$ Shop around. Ask your employer whether you can buy extra coverage through the company's insurer, and use an insurance-premium quote service to compare rates. For a list of competitively priced policies, call TermQuote (800-444-8376), SelectQuote (800-343-1985), or InsuranceQuote (800-972-1104). These services are free, but you might receive solicitations from the insurers whose figures they quote. For a copy of *Life Insurance: How to Buy the Right Policy From the Right Company at the Right Price* (Consumer Reports Books, $11.95 plus $2.50 shipping), call 800-272-0722.

$ For more information. For a free copy of the booklet *A Consumer's Guide to Life Insurance*, send a postcard to the American Council of Life Insurance (Department Consumer, 1001 Pennsylvania Avenue, NW, Washington, DC 20004-2599).

Homeowner's Insurance

Whether you live in a house, an apartment, a condo, or a mobile home, you need insurance to protect your property against fire, loss, theft, or destruction and to protect your assets if someone is injured on your property. When you buy a policy, take a complete inventory of your home and specifically insure certain valuables. You can't collect for the theft of a $10,000 diamond ring unless you can prove it existed. There are several easy ways to save money on a homeowner's or renter's policy:

$ Increase your deductible. Raising your deductible lowers your rates. For example, increasing your deductible from $100 to $250 can cut premiums by 10% on some policies.

$ Ask about discounts. Discounts range from 2% for a simple smoke detector or burglar alarm to 20% for a sophisticated fire/burglar-alarm system. Some companies also offer new-home discounts and reduced rates for nonsmokers.

$ Multi-policy discounts. Ask whether you can get a break on the price if you buy both your auto insurance and your homeowner's insurance from the same company. Compare the policies and prices separately, then factor in the discounts, which can be as high as 15%.

$ Umbrella policies. A good value that few take advantage of is the so-called umbrella liability policy. The more assets you have, the more you have to lose, and the more important it is to have a comprehensive liability policy. It protects against injury done by you or your family members as well as injury that occurs on your property. For about $200 a year, you can get coverage of up to $5 million.

Specialized Insurance

When you buy a car or take out a mortgage or assume any other significant consumer debt, the lender might try to persuade you to buy credit insurance, which covers your payments if you die or become disabled. Credit insurance is a low-value product. Instead of buying specialized policies that cost more, be sure you carry enough life and disability insurance to provide for your financial needs. Don't let lenders bully you. They can't force you to buy a policy as a condition of approving a loan.

Note: See Chapter 7 for advice on choosing health care insurance (page 131), disability insurance (page 134), and long-term-care insurance (page 135). See Chapter 6 for ways to save on auto insurance (page 113).

☐ ☐ ☐

Higher Education

The average cost of a year's tuition plus room and board at a private college is $13,422, according to the editors at *Peterson's Guide to Four Year Colleges*, and that estimate doesn't include extras like clothes, transportation, recreation, and even books. But while it presents a major financial challenge, a college degree still pays off; over a career, the college grad can expect to earn 67% more than a high-school graduate.

With the right financial planning and by taking advantage of financial aid, almost everyone can afford a college education; all it takes is a little research. Because colleges charge anywhere from $25 to $50 to apply, students should weed out unlikely options before they start the application process. The best way to do this is to study brochures, learn about schools from friends and advisers, tour local colleges, and consult guides that compare institutions. Every September *Money* magazine publishes *Money Guide: Best College Buys*. If you can't find it on the newsstand, send a check or money order for $4.50 (payable to *Money Guide*) to Money Guide to College, Box 30626, Tampa, FL 33630-0626. Also, many colleges now supply high schools with informational videos that can save you the cost of a visit.

The Ins and Outs of Financial Aid

The bright side of the high cost of college is that the possibilities for landing some type of aid are good. The more you know about where financial aid comes from and how it is allocated, the better your chances of receiving a larger slice of the pie. Financial aid comes in one of three basic forms—a gift or grant, low-interest loan, or work-study loan—and is usually offered by either the state or federal government, the school, or a private institution. Start by contacting each school's financial-aid office for details about its financial-aid policy—and do it early, so you can meet all the necessary application deadlines. Also, write for a free copy of *The College Money Guide* (Octameron Associates, Inc., Box 2748, Alexandria, VA 22301).

Gifts and grants. Obviously, a gift or grant that doesn't have to be paid back is a student's top choice. Scholarships most often go to the academically or athletically gifted and occasionally to those in need, as is the case with the Federal Pell grants, which are given to students from families with incomes of $32,000 or less. Private colleges also might have endowment money budgeted for grants.

The Army Reserve Officer Training Corps (ROTC) offers one of the best bargains around, as long as you're prepared to repay with service instead of cash. An ROTC scholarship pays up to 80% of a school's tuition (the school often kicks in the other 20%). It also covers room and board and books and supplies plus $100 a month in spending money. Upon graduation, the recipient must serve four years in active duty or eight years in the Reserves or National Guard. Call 800-USA-ROTC to locate a recruiting officer in your area.

Student loans. Government loans such as Perkins Loans and Stafford Student Loans offer below-market interest rates and favorable payback terms, such as grace periods during school years and 10- or 20-year repayment spans. Banks and schools offer similar student loans. Write the U.S. Department of Education (Box 84, Washington, DC 20044) for its free guide, *Federal Student Aid Fact Sheet*. Or call the Federal Student Aid Information Center at 800-433-3243.

Work-study programs. These aid programs are sponsored by the federal government or individual schools and allow students to work—sometimes in a field related to their studies—toward paying college costs. Pay is usually by the hour and at least minimum wage. Also consider applying to a school with a cooperative education program in which you attend school part of the year and work the other part, gaining direct experience in your career field. Contact the National Commission for Cooperative Education (360 Huntington Avenue, Boston, MA 02115; 617-437-3778) for a directory of schools that offer co-op programs.

How to Get the Most Financial Aid

When a student applies for financial aid at a college or university, the amount he or she is offered depends on how much the school costs and how much the student (and the student's family) can pay. What the student and his or her family can pay is a percentage of the family's income and assets determined by a standard formula. When applying for financial aid, your goal should be to adjust your financial picture, within legal limits, to minimize income and assets during the time of applying (and remember, you must reapply for financial aid each year). Here are some pointers:

Don't save in your child's name. A child deemed a dependent is expected to pay 35% of his or her assets toward school fees. Parents are expected to pay only 5.6% of their assets.

Put money into a retirement account. Money invested in an IRA or a 401(k) is not counted as assets. If your account has a loan provision, you'll still be able to retrieve money without penalty later to pay college bills. Ask about loan provisions when you start your retirement account.

Liquidate early. Cash in investments before December 31 of your child's junior year in high school so that the capital gains don't inflate the income that determines the amount of aid you are eligible for.

Where to Find Free Money

More than $100 million in financial aid goes unclaimed each year because students are unaware of many sources for fellowships and scholarships. The College Financial Planning Service (1010 Vermont Avenue, NW, 4th Floor, Washington, DC 20005; 800-933-3100) has a listing of 180,000 sources of funding, including obscure grants to descendants of Confederate soldiers, residents of towns served by the Union Pacific Railroad, and people with the last name Anderson. The group refunds the $45 application fee if you don't receive at least $100 in assistance.

Community and other organizations. Many civic clubs (such as Kiwanis and Rotary), foundations, and churches give education grants. For example, Boy Scouts of America offers a whole list of general scholarships—from partial grants for New England Scouts to the $40,000 Mabel Lawrence S. Cooke Eagle Scout award. Plus, a number of colleges around the country have their own grants for Scouts.

Places of business. Large companies and labor unions often have funds to send children of employees or members to college or technical school. For instance, Philip Morris awards approximately 400 grants averaging $2,000 a year to children of employees. The money goes toward undergraduate, graduate, or vocational training.

Federal Employee Education and Assistance Fund. Children of federal employees and postal workers should apply for funds through the FEEAF. For details, send a stamped, self-addressed business-size envelope to FEEAF (8441 West Bowles Avenue, Suite 200, Littleton, CO 80123).

No-Cost Schooling

Kentucky's Berea College, ranked third-best in the South by *U.S. News and World Report*, is one of several free colleges around the nation. All of the roughly 1,500 students work to help pay tuition and living costs; the difference comes from the school's endowment, gifts, and grants. Write for an application (Admissions Office, Berea College, CPO 2344, Berea, KY 40404). Two other free colleges: Williamson Free School of Mechanical Trade (Office of Admissions, 106 South New Middletown Road, Media, PA 19063) and The Cooper Union for the Advancement of Science and Art (Office of Admissions, 41 Cooper Square, New York, NY 10003).

Free Continuing Education

Many companies encourage employees to continue their education. For example, American Express Publishing pays for up to two job-related classes a semester. The company pays for non-job-related courses, too, if the credits are required for a degree that is related. Ask your boss about similar policies at your company. If no program exists, explain to your supervisor how a course will improve your performance, and see if the company will help pay.

Chapter 10

Enjoying Life

Savings in this chapter...

At last, we have arrived at the best part, the reason we have been pinching pennies in the first place—so that we and our children can enjoy more of the good life. But don't get the wrong idea. Just because you're having fun doesn't mean you can stop saving. Besides, this is one of the best of all areas in which you can save money.

For example, if you're looking for fun, free, educational family entertainment, look no farther than the sky overhead. Many youngsters will be absolutely fascinated by the galaxies dancing in the night sky—and will get a head start on science classes to boot. Although you'd never know it (stargazers congregate in dark fields during the midnight hours), almost every metropolitan area has an astronomy club. Most hold observing sessions for the public. And most importantly, they're usually free. (To receive a listing of clubs and events in your area, send $1 to *Astronomical Directory*, Sky and Telescope, Box 9111, Belmont, MA 02178.)

Thinking about getting a pet? Instead of buying a puppy or kitten, adopt a pet from an animal shelter. Most SPCA shelters charge only a small adoption fee and give the animal several hundred dollars' worth of veterinary care—including all necessary shots and spaying or neutering—before you take it home. In addition, SPCAs typically offer animal clinics and hospitals where prices are generally 25% to 30% lower than standard vet's fees, free behavioral advice, competitively priced dog training, and other services. Check with your local SPCA for details.

Whether you're gardening (page 164), planning a vacation (page 168), entertaining the family, or tinkering at your hobby, part of the fun is figuring out the most efficient ways to get things done, doing as much as possible yourself, and trimming bucks as you go. And hobbies can really pay off before holidays (page 160).

□ □ □

Ten Ways to Save Money and Have Fun at the Same Time

Having fun certainly doesn't have to cost a lot of money. In fact, when they say the best things in life are free, they're talking about laughter, for one. Get into the habit of sharing jokes and cartoons, playing silly games, reading out loud humorous passages from books, and renting funny videos every so often. For a budget outing, go see a high-school sporting event. Here are some more money-saving ways to have fun:

1. Head for water. Buy some old inner tubes—one for each member of your family—at a gas station. Fill them up with air and spend an afternoon floating on a lake or tubing down a river. Pack your own lunch in a cooler. Don't forget an inner tube for it, too.

2. Invite some friends over for dinner and a VCR movie. You'll spend far less than you would going out to dinner and a movie, and when your friends invite you to their place, your entertainment investment will pay double dividends. Turn the heat down, light a fire, and provide blankets for everyone. Make a point to see who can throw the most inexpensive but fun casual get-together.

3. Send a message. Instead of making a long-distance phone call, sit down and write a detailed letter. When you receive a reply, you'll be doubly glad you did. If your kids' grandparents live far away, bridge the distance with a tape recorder. Buy a blank cassette tape and bring your recorder to the dinner table. Have everyone record a message; then you can all sing a song or tell some jokes. Grandma and Grandpa are sure to play it over and over.

4. Make clay. Make a batch of homemade play clay for your kids. Mix together one cup of flour, 1 1/2 teaspoons of alum, 1/2 cup of water, 1 to 2 tablespoons of solid shortening, 1/2 cup of salt, and a few drops of food coloring. When the kids are finished playing with it for the day, store it in an airtight container in the refrigerator.

5. Feed the ducks. Take some stale bread or cereal down to a nearby pond and feed the ducks.

6. Camp out. Next time you feel the urge to get out of town, borrow a tent and go camping in the country. Bring along some marshmallows. Sing songs and tell ghost stories around the camp fire. The kids will love it, and so will you.

7. Wash the car. On a hot day, get your kids together, throw on your bathing suits and flip-flops, and wash the car. While you're all wet, give the dog a bath, too.

8. Go to a reading. It's no wonder that so many writers are poor. They provide some of the best free entertainment in town. Not only do you get to hear new fiction or poetry, but often you receive free refreshments to boot. Check the arts section of your newspaper for listings of readings and lectures.

9. Hunt kindling. Spend an hour in the yard or in nearby woods collecting sticks and small branches. Tie them into small bundles and hang them in your garage or another dry spot. When wintertime comes, simply grab a bundle of kindling every time you make a fire.

10. Catch fireflies. Give each of your children a jar, turn out all of the lights, go out in your backyard and see who can catch the most fireflies. Let them all go.

Pay Less, Play More

If you like to go to the theater, buy a season subscription and save a third of the cost of individual tickets. Or attend preview performances, stand in line for discounted no-show tickets, organize a group of friends and get a group discount, or volunteer as an usher. Subscriptions also save you money on symphony, dance, and opera performances as well as professional sporting events. For even bigger savings, team up with friends to buy an entire season's tickets and divide them up so that you each attend every other or every third performance.

The Library: It's Not Just for Books Anymore

Unfortunately, many people get a bad impression of the public library early on. After all, what school-aged kid wants to spend Saturday writing a term paper, no matter where? But while the library is an invaluable source of information on everything from the American Revolution to Zorn's lemma, it's also much more. The public library is an entertainment center with an incredible range of activities for the whole family. If you haven't been to the library in a while, well, hold on to your hat.

Teaming up with local cultural institutions, libraries across the country now provide art exhibits, poetry and fiction readings, concerts, and dance performances. Many offer lectures, seminars, workshops, and films, often tied to current events. During the 1992 Democratic Convention, for instance, the New York Public Library offered a lecture entitled "Presidential Campaigns Past and Present" and such films as *The Making of the President* and *Primary*.

✔ **Clubs.** The library also provides a great way to meet people and get involved in your community. Check with the librarian to see whether your library has a sewing-pattern or recipe exchange. Ask about clubs and community groups that meet at the library. Or think about starting your own. Many libraries offer meeting space.

✔ **Child care.** One of the library's best services is child care of the highest quality, which—like most things at the library—is absolutely free. Introduce your children to the librarian. She'll do the rest. She'll establish the rules of conduct, explain the available services, and show them how to use the card catalog (or, more likely these days, the computer cataloging system). And then there are the special activities: storytelling, puppet shows, movies, games, and puzzles. Perhaps the kids would like to sign up for a workshop where they'll learn how to make kites, compose a song, write a fable. The library can open up a whole new world for kids, and when the time comes for that term paper, they'll be a step ahead of their peers.

✔ **Everything you ever wanted to know about...** Of course the library still does specialize in books—and plenty of them. You'll find tomes on every conceivable subject. Like to try new cuisines? Check out a cookbook on Thai food or Portuguese pastries. Prefer to visit Portugal instead? The library is filled with travel guides and magazines for every corner of the globe. Thinking of buying a new car? Do some research at the library first—you could save a bundle. The library has resources for just about everything you need to know—from how to find a job to how to pay your taxes. If you can't find what you're looking for, check with the librarian.

✔ **Relaxing.** But don't head to the library just to do research. One of the best places to spend a rainy afternoon is in an easy chair (it's there) in the library's reading room, and it's a great place to take an elderly parent. Browse through the magazines. Find your dream house. Catch up on Hollywood gossip. Improve your golf swing. Request the *New York Times* from December 8, 1941, and read history before it was history. On microfilm, read a critical review of Hemingway before he was HEMINGWAY. If you want, take it home. Use the copy machine to copy the crossword puzzle you missed, the poem you want to remember, or the cartoon you want to pass around.

✔ **Novel fun.** If you want to be the first to read the latest novel, check the book reviews in your local paper. For a quarter, you can reserve your choice at the library. As soon as the book is cataloged, the librarian will call you. When you find an author you love, go back and read everything he or she has written, and throw in a biography at the end. If your taste tends towards the lower end of the literary scale, don't worry about it. Every tenth visit, mix in a classic with your Steel and Dunne. For vacation reading, ask whether your library has long-term summer loans. And if you still want to buy a book, chances are your library has a few for sale—for a quarter or so apiece.

Things You Can Borrow From the Library

- Novels
- Travel guides
- Large-type books
- How-to videos
- Cookbooks
- Biographies, histories, and other nonfiction books
- Language tapes
- How-to manuals
- Records, tapes, and compact discs
- Video movies

Homemade Celebrations

The excitement of a holiday like Christmas, Passover, the Fourth of July, or Thanksgiving lies not only in the festivities of the day itself but also in the anticipation and preparation leading up to it. The easiest way to get everyone in a festive mood is by preparing early for holidays and birthdays. Set aside time to make the cakes and cookies at home, have your children help you make decorations, sew or paint or craft your own gifts.

Instead of shopping for a present, consider giving your spouse a gift of your time and energy, say, a 30-minute back rub every month for the next year, a romantic candlelit dinner, or a hand-knit sweater. Friends and relatives appreciate this kind of gift, too. Offer to baby-sit for an evening, take care of the dog during their vacation, or help clean out the attic. Give a gift of sewing, cooking, woodworking lessons.

Saving at Christmastime

Decorations from the yard. Make decorations from pinecones by spray-painting them silver or gold or adorning them with sequins, tinsel, or ribbon. If the pinecones aren't fully open, put them in a moderate oven for about half an hour.

Homespun ornaments. Make Christmas-tree ornaments from scraps of felt. Holding two pieces of felt together, draw a bell, star, holly leaf, or other holiday motif onto the fabric. If you're not confident about your drawing abilities, use cookie cutters to trace the shapes. Sew the two pieces together using brightly colored embroidery floss and stuff lightly with cotton. Now you can glue on small pieces of felt to decorate each ornament.

Do-it-yourself ornament hangers. Paper clips make sturdy ornament hangers. Just bend out the large part of the clip and place over the branch.

Homemade candles. Buy inexpensive wax (about $2.50 a pound) at a dime store or melt down old candle stubs. Tightly braid cotton string and knot it at each end. To reduce ash and eliminate smoke problems, soak the wicks for at least 24 hours in a solution of one tablespoon salt, three tablespoons borax, and one cup warm water. Then dip them into melted wax repeatedly until the desired thickness is achieved. Color the candles by adding old crayons to the melted wax and stirring thoroughly until color is even (unless you want a swirled effect). For scented candles, add a quarter ounce of herbal oil to each pound of wax.

Making garlands. Popcorn and cranberries are traditional materials for making garlands, but don't stop there. Save wine-bottle corks throughout the year. Use a sharp knife to cut them into disks (you should be able to get 10 or 11 per cork). Spray-paint the disks in festive colors and string them together for a pretty and unusual garland. Or use styrofoam packing disks, dried pasta in interesting shapes—anything that is small and lightweight. For additional holiday decorating and entertaining ideas, check your library for a copy of *A Country Christmas* (Time-Life Books, $15.99) or *Christmas All Around the House: Traditional Decorations You Can Make* by Florence H. Pettit (Thomas Y. Crowell Company).

Presents from your kitchen. Package the dry ingredients for your favorite muffin or cookie recipe, including dried fruit and nuts. Wrap in a pretty paper bag with preparation instructions and a copy of the recipe on an index card. Herb vinegars also make attractive, useful gifts at easy-to-live-with prices. Start with pretty, clear glass bottles, then fill with red or white wine vinegar. Submerge sprigs of fresh herbs, such as tarragon, rosemary, or dill. The herbs will infuse the vinegar with flavor. Add a pretty label and ribbon. For other low-cost gift ideas, see "Shopping for Others: Gift Giving That Won't Break Your Bank," page 11.

It's a wrap. When sending a fragile baby gift, use disposable diapers instead of packing material to protect it. The baby's mother will be doubly thankful.

Collect boxes. Whenever you buy something, ask for a box, even if it's not a gift. By Christmastime, you'll have a variety for packing homemade gifts in.

Beautiful wreaths. Plan ahead: Dry roses and other flowers from your garden during spring and summer and use them to make wreaths and centerpieces at Christmas. A bouquet of dried roses is also a wonderful gift, and an unexpected luxury in December. For a step-by-step guide to making wreaths, look for Richard Kollath's *Wreaths* (Facts on File Publications) at your library.

Make cards. Gather old magazines, scraps of fabric, glitter, glue, construction paper, crayons, and markers, and help your kids make Christmas cards for their grandparents and other relatives. (While you're at it, why not go ahead and make cards for other holidays and birthdays?) A handmade card will certainly be more appreciated than anything bought in a store.

Cut a potato in half, carve a star, bell, or other holiday design into it, and dip it in paint to stamp cards. For other creative ideas, check your library for a copy of *The Art and Craft of Greeting Cards* by

Susan Evarts (North Light Publishers) or *Handmade Greeting Cards* by Maureen Crawford (Sterling Publishing Company).

More Fun and Frugal Holiday Ideas

Toys and games. Homemade toys and games add a special touch to holidays and can personalize a celebration inexpensively. In *The Hanukkah Book* (Schocken Books, $9.95), Mae Shafter Rockland describes how she used cardboard and paint in making a simple board game based on a competitive race from Modi'in to Jerusalem to teach her kids about Hanukkah. You could do the same with any holiday.

Kid power. Kids love to carve jack-o'-lanterns, create May Day baskets, and make valentines. Put their creative energy to use by having them help you make holiday decorations. *The Big Book of Fabulous Fun-Filled Celebrations and Holiday Crafts* (Gladstone Books) by Jim Fobel and Jim Boleach is loaded with ideas and instructions for holiday decorations and food.

Haunted Halloween. Carving jack-o'-lanterns is only part of the fun kids can have with pumpkins. Why not grow your own in the backyard? And when you do, try this trick to create your own masterpiece. A young pumpkin will grow over an object and form a nearly perfect imprint of it. Place a stiff mask under the pumpkin and make a funny or scary face. Use different objects to come up with your own design.

Easter eggs. This Easter, instead of dyeing dozens of real eggs, make papier-mâché eggs that will last for years. Papier-mâché is fun and inexpensive—the two main materials are newspaper and paste. Once you perfect the eggs, why not try your hand at baskets, bunnies, and other Easter decorations? For help in getting started, look in your library for *The Art and Craft of Papier Mâché* by Juliet Bawden (Grove Press). Another helpful guide is *Easter Eggs for Everyone* (Abingdon Press) by Evelyn Coskey. It gives instructions for decorating Easter eggs and includes advice on throwing egg-dyeing parties and Easter-egg hunts and games.

Bargain Birthday Parties

You don't have to spend a lot to throw a fun birthday party for your kids. You just have to know how to have a good time. A simple cake, a few games, and some inexpensive party favors add up to a barrel of fun for children—without breaking the bank. For ideas and advice, look for the following guides in your library: *Happy Birthday Parties!* by Penny Warner (St. Martin's Press), *Birthday Parties for Children: How to Give Them, How to Survive Them* by Jean Marzollo (HarperCollins), and *The Penny Whistle Party Planner* by Meredith Brokaw and Annie Gilbar (Simon & Schuster).

To make the day special, develop traditions that your kids can look forward to. Let them open their presents in bed, pick out what everyone in the family will wear that day, or choose a special birthday meal. It doesn't really matter what it is, as long as it makes the day stand out and is repeated every year.

□ □ □

A Wealthy Harvest

Gardening is a fun and productive way to spend recreational time. As anybody knows who has toiled in the backyard, few things are more satisfying than serving up a salad that you made from scratch. But a recent study found that seven out of every 10 dollars spent on lawn and garden care was wasted. So before you rush out and buy too many seeds and supplies like most amateur gardeners, think about a few things. First of all, a 12-foot-by-12-foot garden is more than big enough for a family of four. Don't plant more than you can consume, give to friends and family, or preserve. And keep in mind that a garden this size requires one to two hours of maintenance per week.

How to Prevent Common Garden Problems

Healthy plants rarely get sick. You can avoid most problems with just a little application of common sense.

1. Beware the bargain. Old fertilizers and pesticides are not going to live up to your expectations. Plants stressed from months on the sales lot, weakened by heat and lack of water or nutrients, might be infested with insects or disease. These are no bargain.

2. Rotate your crops. Even in a small garden rotating helps to confound insects and disease organisms.

3. Don't overfeed. Too much food encourages lush growth (botanical obesity), which bugs love.

4. Water deeply. Thorough watering encourages a healthy root system so that seasonal stress can be better handled by the plants.

5. Use compost as a soil conditioner. You can pay to have the lawn clippings hauled away, then buy fertilizer and peat moss, or you can compost and save two ways. Recycle peelings, clippings, and leaves back into the soil either by burying in the garden or by composting.

6. Know when to fertilize. Apply fertilizer four to eight hours after a thorough watering (the root system is most receptive then). Make sure no fertilizer granules are left to burn leaves.

7. Know when to spray. Don't apply pesticides in the heat of the day. This can burn foliage and flowers or young fruit. And don't apply insecticides while the bees are trying to pollinate your fruit and vegetable crops, because it might decrease your yield.

Savings by Season for the Frugal Gardener

□ Fall □

Leaves. A typical apple tree has up to 100,000 leaves. Sugar maples have 160,000 and large oaks up to 700,000. To cut down on raking costs, consider planting pecan trees in your yard. The pecan's golden-brown autumn leaves disintegrate within about a month of falling. You'll have to collect the pecan nuts, but at least you can eat them.

Maximize brussels-sprout harvest. Brussels sprouts taste better when harvested after a frost or two. Harvest first from the bottom of the plant, removing the leaves immediately above the harvested sprouts. In this manner, you can pick from each plant well into winter.

Bargain shopping. Look for end-of-season plant bargains, especially at nursery chains. But be sure plants are healthy. After depotting, prune any roots that encircle the soil ball.

Store tools properly. With proper care, good tools can last a lifetime. That means keeping wood and metal lubricated and blades sharp to avoid having to use excessive force to get them to function. Make sure all tools are stored properly for winter. Coat them lightly with leftover motor oil or WD-40. Check long handles for cracks, sand out small ones, and coat with linseed oil. If tools have been left out in the rain, coat with linseed oil, which keeps the wood swollen and tight-fitting. Pruning tools need special attention, because dull blades can damage plants. Disassemble hand pruners when possible and hone on a sharpening stone. Put a light coat of oil on the metal.

□ Winter □

Order seeds now to plant soon indoors. Spring will be here before you know it. Some top seed sources: **Bountiful Gardens**, 18001 Shafer Ranch Road, Willits, CA 95490. **The Cook's Garden**, Box 535, Londonderry, VT 05148; $1. **Fedco Seeds**, 52 Mayflower Hill Drive, Waterville, ME 04901; $1. Minimum order of $25. Sells organic gardening supplies too. **Johnny's Selected Seeds**, Foss Hill Road, Albion, ME 04910. **Park Seed**, Cokesbury Road, Greenwood, SC 29647-0001; 803-223-8555. **Thompson & Morgan**, Box 1308, Farraday and Gramme Avenues, Jackson, NJ 08527; 908-363-2225. **W. Atlee Burpee Company**, 300 Park Avenue, Warminster, PA 18974; 800-333-5808.

Houseplants. Exposure to outdoor conditions, however brief, can harm and even kill houseplants. When buying, have them wrapped with paper and stapled shut. At home, keep leaves away from windowpanes on freezing nights.

Prevent winter damage. Keep an eye out for heavy snow on shrubs. By keeping snow from piling up on plants, you'll limit limb damage that can misshape or kill healthy plants. If ice is a problem, use cat litter or sand on walkways instead of salt, which can leach into the soil and kill plants and garden fauna.

Join your area's native-plants club. Being naturally disease- and pest-resistant in their areas, native plants give a region its hardiest specimens.

Planning on growing fresh fruit? Join North American Fruit Explorers (NAFEX), a backyard-fruit-growers' club. The $8 membership fee covers the cost of the club handbook and quarterly publication. For more information, write NAFEX, Route 1, Box 94, Chapin, IL 62628. To join, enclose a check.

□ Spring □

Use your county extension office. Your extension office can tell you the pH of your soil, usually at no charge. (You might need to add lime to temper acidic soil—soil with a pH below 6). The extension can also test levels of nutrients like boron, nitrogen, phosphorus, potassium, and zinc. If you're a vegetable gardener, test for lead, too. Extension agents can advise you once the results are in. Ask for seminar listings, and attend at least one a year for the latest on fertilizers and pesticides. At any good talk, you'll find many ways to improve your garden.

Prepare the site yourself. Instead of renting a Rototiller, skip your daily workout and turn the soil with a pitchfork. This task is less tedious than you think—use your body weight to sink the pitchfork into the ground, then lean back and let gravity do the work. Use the same method to turn your homemade compost.

More peas, please. For better yields and to avoid seed rot during a wet spring, start peas indoors in peat pots about three to four weeks before planting time. As soon as they sprout, plant outside. The head start will pay off nicely.

Disease-resistant plants. To reduce the need for sprays, consider trying these disease-resistant apple varieties: Liberty, Freedom, Redfree, and William's Pride.

Thwart nematodes. To avoid damage to tomatoes by nematodes, microscopic worms that can stunt growth and kill fruit, rotate your tomato crop each year, mulch with shredded bark, and mix in crunched-up eggshells with your tomato-patch soil. The eggshells will promote micro-organisms that feed on nematode eggs.

Cost-effective fence alternative. Before you pay to put up a fence, consider growing a screen. Evergreens make great barriers and are easier on the eyes than the back of a fence. If you don't mind starting out small, they can save you a bundle, too. Consider these, and check your local nursery for the best choices: Dwarf Buford Holly, Foster Holly, Japanese Black Pine, Japanese Cleyera, Leyland Cypress, Nellie R. Stevens Holly, Pfitzer Juniper, Savannah Holly, Thorny Elaeagnus, Upright Juniper, Wax Myrtle.

□ **Summer** □

Double your harvest. To get two heads of cabbage from one plant, when you harvest the first head, be careful not to damage the large leaves next to the ground. In about two weeks, prune all but the largest of the small heads forming around the stem.

Keep tools clean. Fill a bucket with sand and a small amount of used motor oil. After removing soil from garden tools, dip them in the bucket to ward off rust.

Free mulch. Spread a six-inch layer of grass clippings between plants to stop weeds before they start.

Low-impact weed control. Fill a spray bottle with a quarter cup of vinegar per cup of water and spray directly on weeds. To kill weeds around sidewalks and driveways, pour undiluted vinegar into cracks and along edges.

Repairing leaky hoses. Don't buy a new hose because of leaks. If it leaks where it connects at the faucet or the nozzle, you might just need a new washer. You can buy one for about a dime at a hardware store. Pry the old one out with a knife and press in the new one. If the leak is along the length of the hose, buy a mender, a tough plastic tube that fits snugly onto the hose. Cut out the damaged section and reconnect the two pieces with the mender.

Dog food for the dog days. Share your harvest with Rover. Yes, man's best friend will gobble raw vegetables and cooked legumes. Try cooked sweet potatoes, green beans, and squash, raw garlic, and parsley. You'll save on dog food and do your pal a fat-free favor at the same time.

□ □ □

Vacation Bargains

No matter where you go on vacation, there's an expensive way to travel and a bargain way. But getting from here to there on the cheap and staying there for as little as possible—without sacrificing too much on comfort—is a matter that takes some savvy and forethought. If, like most Americans, you prefer to drive to vacation spots, then you should probably be a member of AAA or another auto club and use its services (see page 109). And once you get there, consider reducing food costs by eating your main meal at midday to take advantage of lunch prices and specials. When you eat out at night, look for early-bird dinner discounts.

While you can trim costs no matter where you go, some places were created less expensive than others, and certain activities lend themselves to keeping money in your pocket. Alpine skiing is by nature an expensive sport, while its cousin cross-country skiing is safer, better exercise, just as sexy (if a little slower), and far more affordable. Check out our suggestions for some great destinations (page 172) that offer a maximum of fulfillment for a minimum of cost.

State Travel Numbers

AL: 800-ALA-BAMA	LA: 800-334-8626	OK: 800-652-6552
AK: 907-465-2012	ME: 800-533-9595	OR: 800-547-7842
AZ: 602-542-TOUR	MD: 800-543-1036	PA: 800-VISIT-PA
AR: 800-643-8383	MA: 800-447-MASS	PR: 800-223-6530
CA: 800-862-2543	MI: 800-5432-YES	RI: 800-556-2484
CO: 800-433-2656	MN: 800-657-3700	SC: 803-734-0235
CT: 800-CT-BOUND	MS: 800-647-2290	SD: 800-843-1930
DE: 800-441-8846	MO: 314-751-4133	TN: 615-741-2159
DC: 202-789-7000	MN: 800-541-1447	TX: 800-888-8TEX
FL: 904-487-1465	NE: 800-228-4307	UT: 801-538-1030
GA: 800-VISIT-GA	NV: 800-NEVADA-8	VA: 800-VISIT-VA
HI: 808-923-1811	NH: 603-271-2666	VI: 809-774-8784
ID: .800-635-7820	NJ: 800-JERSEY-7	VT: 802-828-3236
IL: 800-223-0121	NM: 800-545-2040	WA: 800-544-1800
IN: 800-289-6646	NY: 800-CALL-NYS	WV: 800-225-5982
IA: 800-345-IOWA	NC: 800-VISIT-NC	WI: 800-432-TRIP
KS: 913-296-2009	ND: 800-437-2077	WY: 800-225-5996
KY: 800-225-8747	OH: 800-BUCKEYE	

Travel Tips for the Long Haul

Free info first. Contact chambers of commerce, government tourism offices, and state- and national-park headquarters for free trip-planning information.

Road trips. To avoid the high costs of train snack bars or fast-food and convenience stores during long drives, pack a cooler with sandwiches, punch, and homemade snacks. For entertainment, borrow free books-on-tape from your library.

Car-rental savings. If your auto-insurance policy covers rental cars, don't spend extra for temporary coverage. Some credit cards cover insurance fees, too. For more information about saving money while renting a car, see page 115.

Low-cost lodging. Make reservations in advance when possible, and don't forget to ask about discounts; most hotels have lower rates for business travelers, senior citizens, and children.

Stick to a budget. AAA's suggested budget for a family of four is $183 per day for lodging and meals, plus $9 per 100 miles for gas, oil, tires, and maintenance for a car averaging 21 miles per gallon. Don't forget to add for amusements, admission fees, recreation, and shopping.

National Park Passes. If you like to visit national parks, order a Golden Eagle Pass ($25) from the National Park Service (800-365-2267) or any national park that charges a fee. The pass is good for admission to all parks for a year. If you're 62 or older, ask for a free Golden Age passport, which provides free admission and 50% off other fees and services.

Driving south. If you're hitting the highway in the Southeast soon, pick up copies of any of the relevant *Traveler Discount Guides*, which contain dozens of discount coupons for lodgings and tourist attractions. Coupons appear in the order that you'll pass the establishments on the highway. You can get the guides free from participating businesses en route, or you can order them for $2 (to cover postage and handling) from Exit Information Guide Inc., 4205 N.W. 6th Street, Gainesville, FL 32609.

National-park hostels. Apart from being scarce, accommodations in and around America's national parks can cost a pretty penny. Youth hostels in the following parks offer lodging that ranges from $8 to $13 a night (and you don't have to be a youth to take advantage of them): Cape Cod National Seashore, Cuyahoga Valley National Recreation Area, Delaware Water Gap National Recreation Area, Golden Gate National Recreation Area, Point Reyes National Seashore, Redwood National Park. For more information, contact the American Youth Hostel office (733 15th Street, NW, #840, Washington, DC 20005; 202-783-6161).

Budget guided trips. Check with Ramblers Holidays Ltd. (Box 43, Welwyn Garden, Hertfordshire AL8 6PQ, England) and Sierra Club (Sierra Club Outing Department, 730 Polk Street, San Francisco, CA 94109) for well-planned domestic and international trips at good prices.

Flying for Less

When to fly cheap. Weekends are the cheapest days to fly,

From Travel Agents

1. Travel when they want you. Look for cheap fares during annual travel "soft spots": the week after Labor Day, when travelers have returned from summer vacations; the first two weeks in December, before Christmas travel kicks in; the week after New Year's, when the rest of the world is paying off bills.

2. Senior savings. If you're 62 or older, you're eligible for the senior discount coupons offered by most major airlines. Sold in books of four or eight, each coupon is good for a one-way flight within the lower 48 states plus Puerto Rico, the U.S. Virgin Islands, and nearby Canadian cities. Although the coupons do not ensure rock-bottom prices, they do protect you from price hikes.

3. Half-price hotel programs. Membership in one of these programs entitles you to 50% discounts in thousands of U.S. hotels at certain times of year. A trip or two offsets the membership cost ($22 to $100). *Note:* Choose a program not by cost but by location. An extra night or two at half price will more than offset price differences. Call Concierge (800-346-1022), Entertainment Publications (800-477-3234), or Great American Traveler (800-548-2812) to find out about membership privileges, restrictions, and fees.

4. A time for charters. Be extra leery of charter services in winter. If your flight is postponed because of weather, there's no guarantee you'll receive free board and food. Major airlines are required to do this by law, but charters are not.

5. Know before you go. Learn foreign currency exchange rates. If you're traveling abroad, consider countries where you'll receive favorable exchange rates. In Ecuador, a complete dinner for two goes for about $10. In Switzerland, that'll get you a bottle of orange juice.

6. Proper guidance. For tips on low-budget traveling in a specific area, seek advice from a *Let's Go* guidebook (St. Martin's Press) or from one of *The Berkeley Guides* (Fodor's Travel Publications), a new series. While ideal for the young set, both have plenty for anyone on a budget.

7. Think small. Smaller hotels are cheaper and more colorful.

8. Be prepared. Carry your own toiletries. In some parts of the world, these items can be very expensive—especially at the last minute. In a pinch, shampoo does the job for washing clothes, petroleum jelly can serve as a moisturizer or shoe polish, and soap makes a passable shampoo.

9. Rent an apartment. For longer stays, renting can be a good option because you have access to a kitchen.

because the bulk of air travelers are businesspeople flying on weekdays.

Emergency discounts. Some airlines waive advance-purchase requirements and offer up to 50% off the flight price in the event of a death or serious illness in the family. Ask for a "bereavement" fare, and be prepared to show proof of the emergency.

Flying air courier. Flying as an air courier isn't always as glamorous as it might sound. For one thing, you are, in fact, a courier, bearing a package of some sort to a rendezvous of some kind. That means at least a little work is involved. But there's no doubt you can save a substantial amount of money—especially when flying overseas—by taking on such an assignment. To find out about courier-hiring freight companies and courier brokers, along with the potential pitfalls involved, the best source is *The Insiders Guide to Air Courier Bargains* by Kelly Monaghan. Send a check for $14.95 (plus $2 shipping) to The Intrepid Traveler, Box 438, New York, NY 10034.

Caribbean bargain. For adventurous beachcombers, the Caribbean airline Liat offers an island-hopping package that fits even a tight budget. Once you're in the islands, you can get three inter-island flights to any of 20 islands. The off-peak fare (February to June, September to December 15) is $169, and the peak-season fare is only $199. For information, call Liat (800-253-5011, 212-251-1717 in New York).

Eight Great Domestic Vacation Bargains

Within the parameters of a thrifty budget, America offers a lifetime of travel opportunities. Even if you don't choose one of the trips listed here, these should give you a better idea of what to look for.

Georgia: The South, naturally. If walking on isolated sandy beaches and through salt marshes hung with Spanish moss appeals to you, try Cumberland, Georgia's largest offshore island—so beautiful it was once the vacation preserve of wealthy robber barons. The dunes are laced with trails that lead to 120 campsites, mostly in oak and palmetto forests. In terms of amenities, they vary from rustic to even more rustic. All food and supplies must be carried in, assuring money savings here, too. The island is great for fishing, and kids will love spotting feral horses, armadillos, wild turkeys, blue herons, and other wildlife. The only access to Cumberland is via ferry (45-minute trip, $8), which departs from St. Mary's on the mainland. Only 300 people are allowed on the island at a time, and reservations for overnight stays are a must. For free information, contact Savannah Area Visitors Bureau (22 W. Oglethorpe Avenue, Savannah, GA 31499; 800-444-2427).

Louisiana: Rhythms of New Orleans. Any night of the week, any day of the year, crowds of people join the perpetual party in the city's French Quarter. Jazz, blues, brass, zydeco, Cajun, Dixieland: You'll find it coming from all directions. The Crescent City offers urban thrills along with its own mysterious Cajun aura, at Down South prices. But for the best deals, steer clear of the annual events—Mardi Gras (just before Lent) and Jazzfest (late April). Check the free publication *Offbeat* for maps of the music clubs, and *Gambit*, a free entertainment guide, to find out who's playing where. Not all bars have a cover charge, and keep in mind that most make their money on drinks. For traditional New Orleans jazz, attend a show at the historic Preservation Hall (504-523-8939) for only $3. Budget lodging is available at Loyola University, Marquette House, and the YMCA. You'll find plenty of quaint inns priced between $30 and $50. Call the New Orleans/Louisiana Tourist Center (504-566-5031) for information; it also sends out free city and walking maps.

Michigan: Sleeping Bear Dunes. According to local lore, these mammoth sand dunes are a sleeping mother bear waiting for her cubs—the offshore Manitou Islands—to finish their swim. According to geologists, Ice Age glaciers left behind the sandy beaches that now make up Sleeping Bear Dunes National Lakeshore, which extends 34 miles along Lake Michigan, 30 miles from Traverse City. The Interlochen Arts Festival, with guests like Peter, Paul, and Mary and John Denver, is held from late June to mid-August. The park rents canoes during summer and remains open in the winter for cross-country skiing. Stay at Brookwood Home Hostel (616-352-4296), a large cottage that has 12 beds that go for as little as $7 a night. The Victoriana Bed and Breakfast (616-929-1009), an old-fashioned home, includes breakfast and afternoon tea in its overnight rates ($70 per double room). Northwestern Michigan Community College offers dorm rooms during the summer ($25, double). Or call the Michigan Department of National Resources for information on forest camping (616-922-5280). For free information, contact the Traverse City Convention and Visitors Bureau (415 Munson Avenue, #200, Traverse City, MI 49684; 800-872-8377).

Minnesota: Visiting the Twin Cities. Although Minneapolis and St. Paul are hardly twins, they weave a vibrant fabric of culture, art, and history—and most of the sights and sounds are free. Vacation here in summer to take advantage of free outdoor concerts at the Michelob Golden Draft Courtyard (612-724-8437) and at Peavey Plaza at Orchestra Hall (612-371-5600). Buy rush tickets 10 minutes before performances at Guthrie Theater (612-377-2224) for only $6 instead of the regular $34. (Your luck will be best on weekdays.) And visit one of the nation's top modern art museums, the Walker Art Center (612-375-7600), for free. Take a tour of Stroh Brewing Company (612-778-3275). For information about events, pick up *City Pages* or *Twin Cities Reader* (both free). For cheap lodging, rent a room at the College of St. Catherine, Caecilian Hall ($14 per person, per night; 612-690-6604). Another option is Evelo's Bed and Breakfast (612-374-9656), where singles are $40; doubles, $50; triples, $60; full breakfast included. Minneapolis is a Northwest Airlines hub (800-225-2525). For more information, call Visitor Information: Minneapolis Convention and Visitors Association (800-445-7412).

Vermont: Cross-country skiing. If you've got a yen for an adventuresome winter sport but you don't like pricey ski resorts and equipment, cross-country skiing might just be the bargain sport/travel for you. Skis, boots, and poles can be rented for $12 per day versus $50 for downhill equipment, and trail fees are far cheaper than lift tickets. All of the hilly northern states have places to ski. Stay at a cross-country-ski lodge where the trail fee, dinner, and breakfast are included in your lodging rate, and circuit trails mean no backtracking. At the 650-acre Berkson Farm (802-933-2522) in Enosburg, $50 per couple includes breakfast. Two miles from Hazen's Notch, The Inn on Trout River (800-338-7049) has 30 miles of cross-country trails; $43 per person buys lodging and breakfast, and the rate drops each night you stay.

Washington, DC: Government 101. With its many free historical landmarks, Washington, DC, is ideal for prudent travelers. You won't soon forget a romantic after-dark tour of the brightly lit grand monuments and memorials. In the spring, see the sites of DC with the backdrop of a profusion of Japanese cherry blossoms. Many museums—like the National Air and Space Museum and the 14 galleries that constitute the Smithsonian—are located along the periphery of the Mall and charge no admission. Detour from the grassy rectangle, via the Metrorail ($1 to $3.15, depending on distance traveled), to other satellite neighborhoods—like Dupont Circle, where you can catch a free chamber-music or piano concert at the Phillips Collection, the nation's first museum of modern art. Check the *Washington Post* "Weekend" section for other specifics. Speaking of the *Post*, watch the next day's edition come off the presses on a free one-hour tour of the newspaper's headquarters. Reservations are needed a day in advance (202-334-7969). During the summer, you'll find cheap housing at American University and Catholic University. Or try Adams Inn (202-745-3600), a collection of three Victorian townhouses at $55 for a double, or Allen Lee Hotel (202-331-1224), where doubles start at $40.

Washington: The islands of Puget Sound. The San Juan Islands—more than 170 of them between mainland Washington State and Vancouver Island—feature things that money just can't buy: Bald eagles circle above hillsides dotted with farmhouses, pods of killer whales spout offshore, and the sun always shines. Even during the summer months, the islands—which are liberally sprinkled with parks (many with beach access), preserves, and youth hostels—are relatively quiet. You can cruise the back roads without seeing more than a car every hour or so. Marge Mueller's *The San Juan Islands: Afoot and Afloat* is an excellent guide to the area. *The Island Sounder*, the local paper, annually publishes *The San Juan Beckons*, which provides information on island recreation and activities. Friday's Bed and Breakfast (206-378-5848), Snug Harbor Resort (206-378-4762), and Tucker House Bed and Breakfast (206-378-2783) all have rooms starting at around $65. For more information, contact the Washington State Tourism Division (101 General Administration Building, Olympia, WA 98504; 800-544-1800).

The West: Enjoying the national parks. Camping often provides more bang for the buck, but you don't have to camp out to enjoy America's national parks, which are especially good destinations in the West. Take your pick: Rocky Mountains, Zion, Grand Teton, Yellowstone, or Glacier. Hike one of the Rockies' little-known ranges, maybe the Sawtooths of Idaho, the Wind River Range of Wyoming, or the San Juans of Colorado. If you're traveling with a group, make camping reservations in advance by calling the National Park Service (800-365-2267). If you're planning to explore several of the West's national parks during a single year, see page 170 for information about park passes. For a comprehensive listing of parks, fees, and facilities, pick up a copy of *The Complete Guide to America's National Parks* ($12.95), published by the National Park Foundation (1101 17th Street, NW, Washington, DC 20036).

Discovering the Great White North

North of the U.S., the world's second-largest country has plenty of territory to explore. Gas is expensive in Canada, so smart travelers use the extensive public transportation system. VIA Rail, Canada's equivalent to Amtrak, offers scenic routes across the country at bargain prices. Buy your tickets through the Advance Excursion (APEX) program and save up to 40% on a round-trip fare. For transcontinental travel, invest in a Canrailpass ($376), which is valid for 30 days and allows unlimited travel and stops. For information, call VIA Rail (800-561-3949).

□ □ □

A Frugal Finale

The last words...

Now that we've carefully considered the nuts and bolts of saving money in daily life, it's time to take a step back, gaze across the landscape, and put it all in perspective. Being frugal involves more than just following steps to save money, it must become a way of life. You have to blow the breath of your own spirit into the act of being frugal.

Frugality is not synonymous with scroogeness. We penny pinchers have a sense of humor about it all. If you don't think so, just read Jessica King's "Growing Up With a Miser" (page 179). And if you think penny pinching is dull, check out some of the eloquent words it has inspired from such famed thinkers as Winston Churchill and Benjamin Franklin (page 178).

When you adopt frugality, your life becomes richer in all sorts of ways. In "Priceless Ways to Boost Your Marriage" (page 180), we show that romance is a question of spending time, not money.

Finally, let's consider the serious side of penny pinching, the part that goes deeper than just giving us an edge in the competition for a more comfortable life. The Boy Scout Law puts "thrifty" right between "cheerful" and "brave." It says, "A Scout works to pay his way and to help others. He saves for the future. He protects and conserves natural resources. He carefully uses time and property."

That sums it up pretty well. We agree that conserving, saving, and carefully considering the things we use up every day is morally good and good for the environment, and it makes us feel better about ourselves. See "Saving the Environment, Savings for All" (page 182) for a look at the big picture and our last word (for now) on the benefits of frugality.

□ □ □

The Lighter Side of Being Tight: Jokes and Sayings

Lest you think that penny pinching is a bore—or that you will be one if you practice it—heed the words of these sages, to whom frugality was an exalted virtue, and a good source for humor.

"A bargain is something you have to find a use for once you have bought it."
—*Ben Franklin*

"The safest way to double your money is to fold it over once and put it in your pocket."—*Kin Hubbard*

"I finally snapped," the man said. "Last night while I was going over the bills, I discovered how much money my wife squanders, and I hit the roof."

"What did you do?" asked his friend.

"I stormed into the bedroom and gave her a lecture on economy and thrift."

"Did it help?"

"I'll say. Tomorrow we're selling my golf clubs and fishing equipment."

"If you would know the value of money, go and try to borrow some."
—*Ben Franklin*

"Money is better than poverty, if only for financial reasons."—*Woody Allen*

"Saving is a very fine thing. Especially when your parents have done it for you."—*Winston Churchill*

"Just about the time you think you can make both ends meet, somebody moves the ends."—*Pansy Penner*

"With money in your pocket, you are wise and you are handsome and you sing well, too."—*Yiddish proverb*

"A banker is a person who is willing to make a loan if you present sufficient evidence to show that you don't need it."—*anonymous*

> "My son thinks money grows on trees," the overworked businesswoman complained to her secretary one day. "Tonight he's getting a talking-to that'll really get across the value of a dollar."
>
> "How'd it go?" asked the secretary the next morning.
>
> "Not so good," she admitted glumly. "Now he wants his allowance in deutsche marks."

Growing Up With a Miser

Jessica King, one of our editors, describes what it was like growing up with a father who, while generous with family and friends, abhors waste of any kind:
Among other things, growing up with a miser meant waking up early on Saturday mornings to work in the yard, getting around by bus in a city that worships cars, and making do with the attic fan until June (which might not sound so bad, except that I grew up in Dallas, where spring comes in February, and May is downright blistering). Life in our household wasn't easy, but it was never dull.

It took me years to figure out that other fathers did not salvage used computer paper from the office to write home phone messages on. They didn't wear decades-old army pants around the house on Saturdays. They didn't fill up their cars in the morning to take advantage of the overnight condensing of gas molecules. They probably even left the heat on all night in winter.

But that's not to say there aren't advantages to growing up with a parsimonious parent. Who else would pay his daughter a dollar a week to drag the garbage cans to the curb every Tuesday and Thursday so he could avoid the city's $5-a-month charge? What other families in our neighborhood got to save their vegetable peelings for a compost heap? None of my friends' fathers ever sponsored—as far as I know—a family essay contest on Conserving Energy Around the House, with the winner receiving a lobster dinner. And not many of my peers spent their vacations camping in Tyler State Park. (This was never billed as economical—just fun and educational, which it was. It also wasn't Disney World.)

I have to admit that my father comes by his tightfistedness naturally. His mother carried around a big black purse full of rolls and crackers lifted from various restaurants. And my Great Aunt Gladys was a notorious penny pincher, best known for mailing birthday and Christmas cards with the previous sender's name crossed out. Of course, the wrapping paper, too, had that telltale wrinkled appearance.

Like my father, Aunt Gladys had a fondness for buses, but even Dad wouldn't take a bus through the South Side of Chicago at night. That's exactly what Aunt Gladys proposed doing on her 90th birthday. Dad wanted her to take a cab. She was vehement about riding the bus. "Gladys," Dad finally said, "I insist that you take this cab fare."

"I will," Aunt Gladys replied, "but I'm still taking the bus." What did he expect? Any woman who regularly endured the two-day bus ride from Chicago to Dallas was not going to give in to a taxi across town.

Besides, people (at least in my family) adopt a penurious stance early, and it's hard to shake. My sister learned her lesson at a young age. When she was seven, her cat had kittens, and she decided to sell them to the neighbors. She put the kittens in a box, made a sign, and even devised a clever marketing strategy: KITTENS—one for a dime or two for a quarter.

To this day, I can't bring myself to make a long-distance phone call in the middle of the day. Everyone in my office takes notes on clipboards filled with scrap paper, thanks to me. And if I had a car, I'd certainly fill it up in the morning. Instead, I take the bus.

☐ ☐ ☐

Priceless Ways to Boost Your Marriage

In our fast-paced world, it's all too easy to get caught up in the things we must do each day and to lose sight of what's most important to us. We're so busy concentrating on our jobs, our homes, our children that the attention we give to our spouse sometimes takes on a perfunctory note. But it was the little things that built intimacy in the first place: the secrets you shared, the jokes you laughed at, the time you made for each other. It doesn't take fancy trips to Hawaii or expensive anniversary dinners to enhance the romance in your marriage. Just indulge in the activities below, and let the fun you share bring back a spark, a special sense of togetherness, to your relationship.

1. Take a walk in a part of town or a park that you've never been to. Hold hands.

2. Pick a favorite short story or passage from a novel, and read out loud to each other.

3. Put on your pajamas, pop some popcorn, and spend the evening playing your favorite board game.

4. Gather all the photos you have stashed around the house. Sit down together and reminisce about the scene in each photo; then write a funny caption or description of the event on the back.

5. Repeat your marriage vows.

6. Spend a Saturday doing your spouse's favorite hobby together. The next weekend do yours.

7. Check out some travel guides from the library and plan the perfect second honeymoon. Take the time to sketch out all the details: how you'll get there, where you'll stay, what you'll do each day. Just fantasizing about this trip will be fun, but you might also want to start a savings account to make it possible one day.

8. Get up early, pack a thermos of coffee and something to eat, and go on a breakfast picnic.

9. Take turns drawing a portrait of each other. It doesn't matter if you don't have any artistic ability; the important thing is to take the time to really look at each other. Besides, you'll probably both get a good laugh from the final product.

10. Pick a day and switch chores—and any trappings that go along with them, such as aprons and work gloves. At the end of the day, chances are you'll each have renewed appreciation for the other.

Saving the Environment, Savings for All

Each time you shop, your product selection affects the environment as well as your bank account. The key is to reuse as many things as possible. Instead of throwing out household goods, find new ways to use them. When a product runs out of lives, learn how to dispose of it in an environmentally sound way. Here are tips to help you save the planet as well as bucks:

Ditch disposables. Whenever possible, buy the product with a longer life span. Plastic razors, lighters, cameras, cups, plates, and diapers may be displayed on different shelves in the market, but they all end up in the same place—your local landfill. In the U.S alone, 500 million disposable lighters get the heave-ho every year. Stick to the more permanent products, and you'll save money and reduce waste.

The simpler, the better. Buy in bulk, and give serious consideration to the amount and type of packaging a product carries. Packaging accounts for 10% to 15% (and sometimes up to 50%) of a product's cost and 40% to 50% of consumer waste.

Choose the right paper products. Look for Marcal paper products—bathroom and facial tissue, napkins, paper towels—at your supermarket. They're 100% recycled, *and* they're 15% to 25% cheaper than Charmin or Bounty.

Examine detergent use. Phosphate, the chemical often used to soften water and prevent dirt from being redeposited on fabric, eats up oxygen in lakes and streams. Check the ingredients on your detergent container, and use only low-phosphate or phosphate-free detergents. (Liquid detergents are generally phosphate-free.) Also use less detergent. According to *Consumer Reports*, manufacturers recommend using more than is really necessary. For information on detergents, send a self-addressed, stamped envelope to The Ecology Center (2530 San Pablo Avenue, Berkeley, CA 94702). Ask for the detergent fact sheet.

Stop the flow of plastic. Steer clear of short-lived plastic toys and trendy electronic gadgets. Pass up the Ninja Turtles for more traditional, long-lasting toys like wooden blocks, marbles, and jacks. These toys will mean more to your kids in the long run, and your kids can hand them down to their children.

Liberate your mailbox. According to the U.S. Postal Service, every man, woman, and child in the United States receives an average of 248 pieces of junk mail per year. By eliminating your name from mail listings, you'll be saving trees and limiting temptations. To have your name removed from mailing lists, write to the Mail Preference Service (Direct Marketing Association, Box 9008, Farmingdale, NY 11735-9008). Tell credit- and charge-card companies, magazines, and the mail-order companies whose catalogs you *do* want not to include your name on the lists they rent out.

Recycle motor oil. Experts say that 2.1 million tons of motor oil seeps into rivers and streams each year. Considering that a single quart of motor oil can pollute 250,000 gallons of drinking water, that's a lot of contamination. What can you do to prevent this? Most communities have an oil-recycling collection program. Call local gas stations or the state environmental department to find out where the nearest recycling site is.

Return bottles and cans. Return bottles and aluminum cans and receive money in exchange. It makes sense for everyone.

Want to recycle paper at home? Making paper is fun and economical. You can create a whole slew of paper textures and colors using various kinds of papers and decorations like dried flowers or leaves. For instructions, contact the National Recycling Coalition (1101 30th Street, NW, Suite 305, Washington, DC 20007; 202-625-6408).

□ □ □

The Editors

In addition to *The Penny Pincher's Almanac*, **Dean King**, **Jessica King**, and **Logan Ward** write and edit *The Southern Farmer's Almanac*, *Traditional Country Christmas*, and *The Movie Renter's Handbook*. Originally from the South, all three currently live and save in New York City.

———————

Additional Contributors

Hank and Marlene Bruce are the authors of *Garden Trivia* (Quinlan Press). They live in Sorrento, Florida, where they write frequently about gardening.

Winifred Conkling, co-author of *Get in Shape, Stay in Shape* (Consumer Reports Books), was an editor at *Consumer Reports* for six years. Currently she is working with consumer advocate Esther Peterson on her memoirs.

Geoffrey Morris is executive editor of *National Review*, where he has written about, among other things, how the federal government can trim *its* budget.

Bart Mullin is an antiques dealer and fiction writer who lives in Charleston, South Carolina.

Richard Nalley, a nationally syndicated wine columnist for Copley News Service, has published articles on wine and food in *Gourmet*, *The New York Times*, and *Travel & Leisure*.

Elizabeth Perkins is a certified interior designer and illustrator, who lives in Richmond, Virginia.

Julie Reed, who lives and teaches in New York City, is the health editor of *The Southern Farmer's Almanac*.

Kirk Walsh, a freelance writer, lives in New York. Her articles and product reviews have appeared in *Rolling Stone*, *Discover*, and *Seventeen*.